About the author

Alex Atherton is an experienced educator, award-winning keynote speaker and leadership coach.

His professional background was in education. He spent 25 years working in inner-city comprehensive secondary schools, over half of which was as a headteacher in London.

He speaks about generations at conferences and events across the country and trains organisations in how they can recruit, retain and engage Gen Z.

Alex's coaching clier   ship teams, from a variety of ʒ

Outside of work, he i   s his time with both. He also sı   thin, likes his music loud and h   ɔnes.

Originally from Yorkshire, hɔ ....

CW01497184

Contact via
alex@alexatherton.com
www.alexatherton.com

https://www.linkedin.com/in/alex-atherton/

THE SNOWFLAKE MYTH

Explaining Gen Z in the workplace and beyond

A guide for leaders, managers and parents

ALEX ATHERTON

The manufacturer's authorised representative in the EU
for product safety is Authorised Rep Compliance Ltd,
71 Lower Baggot Street, Dublin D02 P593 Ireland (www.arccompliance.com)

Troubador Publishing Ltd
Unit E2 Airfield Business Park,
Harrison Road, Market Harborough,
Leicestershire. LE16 7UL
Tel: 0116 2792299
Email: books@troubador.co.uk
Web: www.troubador.co.uk

ISBN 978 1836284 710

British Library Cataloguing in Publication Data.
A catalogue record for this book is available from the British Library.

Printed and bound in the UK by imprintdigital.com.
Typeset in 11pt Futura PT Light by Troubador Publishing Ltd, Leicester, UK

for Clare

Young People have exalted notions, because they have not been humbled by life or learned its necessary limitations; moreover, their hopeful disposition makes them think themselves equal to great things – and that means having exalted notions. They would always rather do noble deeds than useful ones. Their lives are regulated more by moral feeling than by reasoning – all their mistakes are in the direction of doing things excessively and vehemently. They overdo everything – they love too much, hate too much, and the same with everything else.

Aristotle
4th century B.C.

Contents

Preface   xi
Introduction   xxi

PART ONE: LEARNING FROM THE PAST   1
Chapter 1:   Generations: Who Belongs Where?   3
Chapter 2:   Every Generation Faces the Same Issues   24

PART TWO: TODAY'S GEN Z MYTHS AND
    MISUNDERSTANDINGS   37
Chapter 3:   The Myth of Lazy   39
Chapter 4:   The Myth of Unreliable   69
Chapter 5:   The Myth of Instant   114
Chapter 6:   The Myth of Apathy   141
Chapter 7:   The Myth of Slack   161
Chapter 8:   The Myth of Fake   181

PART THREE: LOOKING TO THE FUTURE   203
Chapter 9:   What Does the Future Hold for Gen Z?   205
Chapter 10:   Leaving Your Legacy   221

Acknowledgements   233
Further reading   235
Working with me   236

Preface

What happens near an exam hall during those final 15 minutes prior to start time tells you a lot about a secondary school.

"Have you revised? I haven't done anything at all for this one!"

"Me neither. I didn't even know which subject it was until this morning. I am going to fail SO BADLY."

From experience, I know that the students who say they have done no revision are never quite telling the truth. They have done some, possibly even plenty. Bragging about what you have not done can be a useful method of calming the nerves.

I was not particularly interested in conversations like this. My interest was in those who were silent. This would be the case for one of two reasons. The first was that they had done their work and just wanted to get in the room. The second reason was that they really had done nothing. Their silence came from the grim reality hitting them before the ordeal. Flashbacks to all the times when their parents and teachers had tried to persuade them to go another way would run through their heads. Often, these would be the brightest kids. They knew they were able and had always been told as much. When it came to it, they thought they could go through the gears and perform.

Days like these defined the initial years of my career. As a teacher first, then secondary school headteacher, I watched with increasing bewilderment as a series of high-performing students would throw it all away. The sobering moments watching them open their results envelopes in August were no better.

The role of a secondary school headteacher was difficult, but I loved it. The pressures were considerable, particularly amongst the challenges of the large inner-London comprehensives I ran, but I enjoyed working with young people and trying to make a difference to their lives.

When I started teaching in the mid-'90s, attitudes to external examinations were broadly similar to those I had experienced as a student. My own secondary education was a world away from the schools I worked in, but the traits of many students and teachers were similar.

The concept of publishing school examination results was still new, as was the practice of organising the data into league tables. There was an edge of accountability. The school I joined as a rookie teacher had been inspected recently, which led to the departure of a number of staff. That edge was very blunt compared to today. Many teachers arrived in September not knowing how their classes had fared in GCSE and A level examinations. The results primarily belonged to the students rather than to the school. Much would depend on the support of their families.

For the first period of my career, there were many students who worked hard, particularly in the run-up to exam time at the end of the academic year. They wanted to succeed, to make themselves and their family proud. They were driven, even if some of their teachers were not. There were also many who were indifferent about how they did. These would make a point of doing as little as possible so they had an excuse down the line for the state of their grades. This would be reflected in the effort they put into their lessons and homework, or lack thereof.

A lack of revision was not the only way in which high-performing students would throw away their future prospects. The rite of passage of 'leaving school', despite the fact their post-16 studies were mere months away, might involve clearing local shops out of eggs and flour, then depositing it all over the buildings and each other. Once was enough, but it could go on for weeks in the run-up to the exams.

Every year, a new set of 13-year-old girls would emerge as the smoking group. The signs were generally there earlier than this rebellion, but the cigarettes were the most persistent manifestation several times a day. It got worse at school discos as teenagers would often arrive under the influence of alcohol, then surreptitiously pass around small bottles of spirits. 'It's what they do when they're young' was the culture of the time. And in an age before smartphones and widespread use of CCTV, there was no record of it.

There came a point when all this started to change. Large numbers of students wanted to stay late, and often very late, after school to revise or finish their coursework. They wanted more on Saturday mornings and during school holidays. The smoking group did not emerge. School absence was more or less cut in half.

It is hard to pinpoint exactly why and how. Government aspirations that standards in comprehensive schools could rise significantly started to yield results. The accountability culture, expectations of both staff and students and the means of spreading best practice all represented a paradigm shift from the beginning of my career. I found myself on the cusp of this as a new headteacher of a secondary school in Tottenham, London. This was a part of the city where there was everything to do and an expectation that it could happen.

From my perspective, the shift was about more than this, and it continued over the course of my years running schools. Increasing numbers of students had a real hunger for success. They worked hard with their teachers to reach their ambitions. One after another became the first of the family to go to university and to keep succeeding when they got there. As the years of austerity in the early 2010s kicked in, despite making it difficult, the tough economic conditions often acted as a spur.

Some of those examination results days were the favourites of my whole career. Screams of delight and tears of joy from students, their families and their teachers indicated years of hard work paying off. The queue to collect grew ever longer. Fewer wanted to arrive long after everyone else had gone so they could learn the scale of their personal disaster in private.

I left my last headteacher post in 2018 and slowly moved away from the world of running schools. During this period, I started to notice that the generation of young people I had been responsible for in schools were being described in very different ways by newspapers, in the media and by my peers. It took a while for me to realise that this was becoming a trend. 'Young people aren't what they used to be' is a popular line to take, but it was only when I saw a clutch of headlines in quick succession that I realised the issue was not going away.

I am talking about headlines like this:

> Melting under the pressure! HALF of managers complain it's 'difficult' to work with snowflake Gen Z employees – while more than a THIRD reveal they've had to FIRE younger staff because they're too 'easily offended'.[1]

Gen Z workers are terrifying bosses with woke demands. Junior at start up called boss on weekend to demand BLM support while others assign tasks to their bosses, and demand PTO for 'anxiety'.[ii]

Millennials and Gen Z really ARE snowflakes: Scientists find people aged 18 to 25 are the most upset when they're labelled narcissistic, entitled and oversensitive.[iii]

Rise of social media has 'turned university students into snowflakes.[iv]

You might think that all this was coming from a particular corner of the British printed press popular among an older demographic. There is more than a hint of truth about that. If comments of this nature had only come from that particular element of the media world, I would not have worried so much. Keen though I was to see the HR procedures that allow for employees who are 'too easily offended' to be dismissed, it was also difficult to take this seriously. It presented as a prime example of older generations not seeking to understand.

When I heard my own peers talk about the issues they were having in their workplaces, my eyes really opened. It was not accompanied by the kind of culture war rhetoric prevalent in sections of the press and social media, but it did represent a genuine dissonance from my own experience.

Gen Zers were just clueless, I was told, and lazy and entitled with it. Under the slightest deadline pressure or being pulled up for their performance, they would off sick with a mental health issue. They picked up their bags, left on the dot and would not think twice about moving from a job that had invested heavily in their professional development.

The Snowflake Myth

It got to the point of ridicule with comments such as, "Who do these people think they are? They have only worked there for a year and now they want to go part time!" Or, "They simply do not understand that they have to put in the evenings and weekends to get anywhere at all."

Then came my coaching clients. One after another told me that they were struggling to recruit, retain, motivate and understand young members of staff. Then, in the next sentence, they would say they were sick and tired of dealing with their 'snowflake young staff'.

My mood progressed from bewilderment to anger. The smart, ambitious and dedicated kids I had led worked harder at school than any previous generation I knew, including my own. Many of my peers seemed to have selective memories of their behaviour as students or young professionals. There was a fixed view of what it was like to be young, and how professionals in their formative years should expect to live their lives and be treated.

At first, I questioned myself and my work in education. What had I got wrong? There is a long answer to that question, and it is covered at various points across this book. The short version is that there is much the education system in England, and doubtless elsewhere, can do differently to prepare young people for adult life.

I also questioned whether my perception really had been wrong. I compared year group cohorts across my career and remembered what it was like to work with them. In the end, despite the fond memories I have of all of them, there was no contest. The Gen Z cohorts were way ahead.

My view hardened over time that the issues were not with Gen Z, but with the members of the older generations who did not wish to take the time to understand them or their outlook. There was a distinct lack of reflection, including about why Gen Z might not have the same values or want the same outcomes as their predecessors. This played out in the workplace too, as new employees arrived with different expectations about how their professional development should operate and what might constitute a reasonable career trajectory.

Since I started making these observations in 2018, recruitment and retention problems have only worsened for many employers and industries. There are genuine problems to solve. I found myself increasingly engaged in conversations with employers from one line of work after another about the teenagers I had worked with and what my peers might do differently.

Eventually this morphed into a research project, a talk I have given to many audiences, and then this book. Through the talk, I have come to describe myself as the person who explains Gen Z to Gen X.

In *The Snowflake Myth,* I will define the different generations in some detail, including the dates for who belongs in those generations. At this point, I must stress that while 'explaining Gen Z to Gen X' is a good tagline, I know my audiences include people from every generation old enough to work. This book is ultimately about attitudes and experiences, not age. If you are reading this, I hope you will find lessons relevant to any intergenerational relationship.

At the end of my talk, people ask questions, come up and talk to me, or connect online to take the conversation further. I am told that my work has an impact. Parents of grown kids in their twenties tell me I have helped them understand their sons and daughters much better. These parents often want to test the waters about their kids' recent career decisions or what their next move might be, as though we're back in a school parents' evening. Leaders and managers tell me of the strategies they are now going to employ to find, keep and motivate the best and brightest. Most gratifying of all, Gen Zers tell me that I have made them feel heard and seen in a way that would never have happened if they had made the case themselves. 'It felt like you were talking about me' is the best compliment I could ever receive.

My personal hope for this book is that I can spread this understanding a little wider.

I would like:

- Decision-makers and managers in organisations to understand the youngest generation in the workplace better, see the world through Gen Z's eyes, and thereby enable leaders to recruit, retain, engage and motivate much more effectively.
- Parents of Gen Z to understand their offspring better, should that be an issue, and have better relationships.
- Generate more empathy towards Gen Z, particularly as the remainder of this cohort enters the workplace.
- Some Gen Zers to pick up this book and find enough meaning within it that they hand it to their employer and ask them to read it, so that their working experience can improve.

I am well aware that Gen Z is not looking for an advocate to speak out on their behalf. Even if they were, I very much doubt they would choose me. The starting point for this book was that I wanted my own generation to hear a different message.

In my focus groups, it was consistently the case that Gen Z members were interested in how the cards they have been dealt compared to previous generations. They also seem to be interested in someone prepared to give what can be a difficult message to his Gen X peers, which might be listened to more closely than if the younger generation gave that feedback. I also hope that Gen Z might understand the older generations a little better as a result of this book, and that it equips them for improved relationships in work and family settings.

Finally, I hope that at least a few of the students I worked with in their teenage years stumble across this book and find that their secondary school headteacher is still out there rooting for them, whatever they make of my conclusions.

Introduction

If I told you that 50% of your Gen Z workers anticipate leaving their job in the next 18 months, what would that mean for your company? At the same time, since reports show Gen Z is 64% less productive than Gen X, how are you going to fill that gap?

Gen Z's engagement with the traditional workplace is frequently different to their managers' expectations. For the most part, *The Snowflake Myth* will focus on the issues faced by employers and how to explain and resolve them. From my experience of talking to audiences, the explanations and resolutions for those issues are of interest to parents too, even if indirectly.

Let's start by taking a look at the current landscape.

1. *'64% less productive than Gen X or Boomers'*

A January 2024 survey by Vitality[v] revealed that 'Gen Z employees reported an average of 60 days of lost productivity, compared to 36 days for Gen X and Baby Boomers' – a stark 64% difference.[vi] 'Lost productivity' is the combination of sickness absence and days where those surveyed 'struggled to achieve anything in the office'. This was due to 'poor mental health, including burnout, stress, insomnia and obesity'.

2. '50% of Gen Z workers expect to leave their job within the next 18 months'[vii]

This survey showed the challenges of both retention and managing a multi-generational workforce. The percentage of Gen Z workers who expected to move on in this period of time was far higher than for other generations. Almost twice as many Gen Z put themselves in this category compared to Gen X (28%) and Boomers (29%). The latter figure is amplified by the fact that some of the Boomers surveyed would have been near retirement. At 38%, the Millennials figure falls in between, but the Gen Z figure remains almost a third higher.

3. A quarter of a million Gen Z in the UK are 'running their own business'

The UK has never had more businesses, and the numbers of Gen Zers who are running them is growing very quickly. In January 2024, 243,000 were named as directors at Companies House.[viii] This was a 42% increase on the previous year where the figure was 171,000. Given that, it is more than reasonable to work on the basis that the number is now through 250,000 and possibly closer to 350,000. If it continues at this rate, it will be well over a million by 2030. The numbers of Gen Z operating as directors has made recruitment harder. Since this key alternative to a 'regular job' has grown, there are fewer young staff available to the job market.

4. '45% of hiring managers say that Gen Z is the hardest generation to work with'

A 2024 survey[ix] put Gen Z way ahead of other generations in terms of both how 'challenging' they are to work with and how 'difficult to manage' they are. Gen Z was considered to be five times as difficult as Boomers (9%), more than three times as difficult as Gen X (13%) and three-quarters more difficult than Millennials (26%).

5. '69% of Gen Z say middle management is too high stress, low reward'

Gen Z is saying no to middle management[x] with a majority not wanting to do it. 'Conscious unbossing' is a problem for organisations who have managed to recruit and retain young staff, but then discover a significant issue with succession planning. Approximately 90% of employers 'still think that middle managers play a crucial role', but 72% of Gen Z would 'rather choose an individual route over managing others'.

6. '67% of Gen Z say that they 'should only do the work they are paid for[xi]''

Gen Z's engagement with work, and the concept of going 'above and beyond' in particular, is low. The figure above (for 18-29-year-olds in 2022) was approximately a third higher than for those in their thirties and forties, almost twice than those in their sixties.

Quiet quitting[xii] is when an employee gradually disengages from their job over time, without deliberately bringing it to the attention of their manager or anyone else. 'Working to rule' is a variation on a theme, but quiet quitting describes the continuous process of reaching that point. Organisations and their leaders have a whole series of problems as a result. The general headings are obvious and have been named already, but there is a mixture of other issues underneath them. The sub-points below are intended as a representative sample.

a. Recruitment

i. Organisations cannot fill posts essential to the day-to-day operation of the business.

ii.   Recruitment costs are high, and become higher when advertisements require a bigger budget, or when selection processes have to run several times before a successful appointment.

iii. Morale dips because of the additional work carried out by unhappy, understaffed teams.

iv.   Productivity, efficiency and quality control suffers, and some staff members experience burnout.

v.   Plans for expansion are put on hold or abandoned altogether.

vi.   Orders are delayed or cannot be met, thereby having a reputational impact.

vii. New orders cannot be taken on, leading to a loss of both custom and market share.

viii. Staff costs increase because agencies are used to cover the shortfall.

ix.   Attention and resources move away from product development, training or innovation in order to meet urgent demands.

b. Retention

i.   Recruitment costs rise further as 'successful' appointments only last for a short period of time.

ii.   Training costs rise, and resources are wasted, when recently onboarded staff decide their future is best served elsewhere.

iii. Experienced members of staff spend an increased proportion of their time in mentoring and supporting new recruits, taking them further away from their main responsibilities.

iv.   Handover, should it be possible at all, and client relationship development take up more time.

v.   Team cohesion breaks down as strong working relationships are repeatedly disrupted by turnover.

vi.   Reputation is put at risk if existing employees leave in negative circumstances and choose to publicise their experience online.

Equally, customers may become frustrated in dealing with constantly changing points of contact who lack historical context.

vii. Employees can take clients, other contacts and inside knowledge with them, even if they have only been in post for a short period of time.

viii. Ongoing issues with turnover can damage industry perception of the organisation if advertisements for the same posts continue to appear.

ix. Staff who had not considered their future start to do so when they see others who have benefitted from moving to a new role.

c. Engagement and motivation

i. Low levels of productivity affect the bottom line. It can also lead to a company under pressure from customers to hire more staff than it really needs.

ii. HR spends more time resolving casework, including grievances and disciplinaries.

iii. Employees spend more time complaining about the business than contributing towards it.

iv. The quality of the final product suffers as disengaged workers are less concerned about maintaining high standards.

v. Staff are less likely to take the initiative and solve problems themselves because it is 'above their paygrade', leaving them to managers who are already overworked.

vi. Innovation suffers as members of staff carry out their jobs without seeking to contribute to the organisation beyond their job description.

vii. Sickness absence not only increases but becomes a vicious circle as the absence of some staff creates more workload for others, who then need time off themselves.

viii. Office politics become worse, along with a general slide into a more toxic culture.

ix.   Staff check their messages less frequently, leading to breakdowns in communication.
x.   Cliques develop as team collaboration breaks down.

It is not a great set of affairs, is it? Yet the competition faces same issues. I do not claim to have a silver bullet to resolve all this. However, the ideas, strategies and evidence presented in this book should put you in the best possible position to deal with what is in front of you. The statistics listed above demonstrate the issues, but also the opportunities for a new way forward.

Who am I to write this book?

My professional background and life experiences put me in a good position to help you solve your version of the problems I've just outlined.

My teaching career had what I can only describe as a stuttering start, and that's being generous. The fact that the vast majority of my degree was in government and politics[1] offers a strong clue that I did not have teaching in mind as a career. My first application for a PGCE (Post Graduate Certificate in Education) was rejected by Manchester Metropolitan University. I remember thinking that was a fair decision at the time, given I had been completely stumped by the icebreaker question 'why do you want to be a teacher?' This gave the interviewers the clear impression that I had not really thought it through. I wonder what comments were made about 'young graduates these days' in the aftermath.

---

1   I did the marvellous BA (Econ) at Manchester University. In addition to government and politics, I studied economics, econometrics (the mathematics element of economics), social policy, sociology, and social anthropology. Following my initial failure to get into teacher training, I then did a master's degree in political theory. Not much to suggest teaching was a vocation for me is there?

A year passed before I got on the PGCE course at Leicester University[2], but at the end of the year it took me five attempts to get my first teaching job. Failures included one headteacher telling me that they could not understand my accent (trust me, it is not strong; if you listen carefully, you might hear Yorkshire, but I wouldn't get a part in *The Full Monty* or *Kes*), and not getting the job in a school where I had done my second teaching placement (these days, you would have to be seriously bad not to succeed in those circumstances).

I was also unsuccessful for a job where the headteacher who interviewed me had to resign several months later after reports of a scandal in the press. He was caught in a sting operation when it emerged he was fond of getting prostitutes to dress up in the school uniform. The *Daily Mirror* arranged for such an encounter and the headteacher left his post in a hurry.

To be fair to me, it was particularly competitive to get on a social science PGCE course, or at least that is what I was told. Although much of my time in schools involved teaching 'what was left over that others do not want to do', a high proportion of my lessons were with sixth form students who were becoming young adults and readying themselves for life beyond school. For decades, I worked with young people in the midst of figuring out whether they wanted to go to university, hit the job market or take some time off if they were fortunate enough to be able to do so. They wanted to know more

---

2   At the time, I remember thinking this was a bit of a result. Manchester Metropolitan was still known as the 'old poly(technic)' and seen as a step down from the original university. Polytechnics gained university status in 1992. Leicester University was viewed as a 'proper' university, as opposed to its upstart younger sibling De Montfort, which had the indignity of campuses in places like Milton Keynes. I do not recall such snobbery fondly, but it seemed to matter to a lot of people back then.

about what their young professional life might be like, where it could be, what property they might be able to buy and when.

Once I got into a school, things started to happen quickly. As I did not work in a core subject department, there were no other teachers to manage, and the pastoral responsibilities were sewn up by those who had no plans to move on for a very long time. I found my way through as the 'exams guy' first and then the 'data guy'.

I came into schools at a time when my alleged data skills made me the one-eyed person in the land of the blind when it came to assessing a school's performance. I am old enough to remember not only when 'league tables' did not carry much prominence, but when some schools did not even add up their results either. Positions had to be published by the government for the school to know how it had performed. When teachers came back to work in September, they got on with the serious business of comparing their tans, not looking at the examination results of their classes. There was little sense of accountability. I did not make myself popular with some by completing the analysis that made it possible.

Following that, I was successful in each of my first attempts to be assistant headteacher (at age 27), deputy headteacher (at 30) and headteacher (at 33). That was a pretty hot streak considering how it started.

The relevance of that to this book is I know what it is to be a young professional trying to get going and finding that both the organisation and profession I had joined could be indifferent to change. I remember some level of indignance from colleagues around having to do any professional development at all, in teaching new content in the summer term when the sun was out and in engaging with some kids who, on the surface at least, did not want to know. All of this seemed very important to me.

I am pretty sure that I was seen as different, perhaps even representative of a new wave wanting to see change that was not welcomed by everyone. My views on stress, rewards, workload and productivity were not the same as the generations ahead of me.

Impatience for progression

The same applies to my levels of patience about the speed at which I should move through the profession. I should stress that I had no plans to become a headteacher. When I was asked by colleagues early in my career if I would ever want to do it, I would give a glib answer on the lines of 'perhaps in my late forties', which was a chasm away at the time. The fact I taught a minority subject meant I had no clear way through as a head of department, for example, because there was no team of teachers to lead.

Although I had no road map for career progression, I did not take kindly to any idea that length of experience alone should be the guiding criterion for when I might progress. The same arguments I hear from my peers in various industries today about Gen Z's expectations for promotion were applied to me as well.

I know what it is to make ambitious moves for roles I was told I did not have the experience for, to be met with cynicism when I could see a better way of doing things and to be told that I would be 'wasted' in education and should have made another choice. These are all statements that could easily be made by a Gen X to a Gen Z now.

In a few job interviews over time, I found myself saying that I knew my CV could present as though I was only interested in getting promoted, and racing through the system as quickly as I could. The truth is that I found myself in circumstances where I was either looking to move geographically or to a new workplace, and opportunities came my way which I neither expected to arrive nor expected to be successful in gaining.

Although for obvious reasons I will focus on Gen Z in this book, I also taught the older generations. Before the eldest Gen Z reached secondary school, I was the headteacher of many Millennials. Some sixth form students in my earliest teaching days were born in the late 1970s and are Gen X, the same as me. They are currently in their late forties. In between them and the first Gen Zs to arrive at secondary school came many cohorts of Millennials. They experienced the 'revolution', as it felt at the time, of text messaging, dial-up internet and the Star Wars prequels. I was part of a trainee teacher cohort who opened our mouths in shock the first time our teaching was interrupted by a student receiving a phone call during a lesson.[3]

I refer to this because I am in a position to compare the experience of generations over time, born between the late 1970s and the late 2000s. There were over 10,000 students from various generations I had responsibility for, either as a senior leader or headteacher, with the large majority during the latter role.

You may read this thinking a headteacher like me would have been busy in my office all day and I would not have known many of the students. It is true that I did very little classroom teaching once I was a headteacher, but it is not true that I had little to do with the students. It was really important to me to get out and about and engage with them. I am not claiming that I knew every name or every individual, but I did have a strong relationship with the student body and dedicated my working life to them.

In addition to that, I interviewed and employed hundreds of young professionals. As a senior leader and as a headteacher, I had

---

3   The sheer incredulity of it. We all shared that story with our friends beyond education as though the world was coming to an end.

responsibility for their professional development, career opportunities and welfare.

I have not relied on my experience alone to write this book. My research has included a range of focus groups with Gen Z young professionals, an extensive set of secondary sources and the feedback and follow-up from every audience in front of which I speak. The best way of describing it is that my professional background has given me the context and desire to proceed, but the vast majority of the content has come from the ongoing research.

I might be biased, but I am also convinced that the generation of young people who went through the schools I led worked harder, were more ambitious and were the most outstanding set of young people we have ever produced. They have also faced, and continue to face, extremely difficult challenges bequeathed to them by older generations who could have done better.

Earlier in this introduction, I established the key problems employers are looking to solve. There is a further perspective. As older generations, we are also reliant on younger people to shoulder the burden of solving some enormous problems.

The legacy left for Gen Z

The first of these problems is climate change. There have been many times over the course of my research where I have been asked by Gen Zs whether my generation was educated about the prospect of climate change and its likely consequences. Despite the selective memories of some of my generation, the answer to that question is yes. The uncomfortable truth is that the evidence around climate change has been around for a long time.

The Snowflake Myth

The question that follows is always: "Why hasn't your generation done anything about it?" It is a fair question and I do not have much of an answer for them. The typical response is that my generation has had their chance, ducked it, and so Gen Z will need to take it from here. Gen X is requested to back away from the area and leave them to get on with it. Given the health difficulties ever rising temperatures could cause in Gen X's later lives, we will need them to be successful.

Secondly, the issue of an ageing population. I have never been convinced that there would be a state pension should I reach that age. I also recognise that even if it does exist, I am unlikely to be relying on it to the same extent as the vast majority. More significantly, to me at least, is having a functional National Health Service (NHS) and adult social care becoming a higher priority for public spending than is currently the case. Given the demographics over time, which I go into during Chapter 5, this issue is growing considerably.

I was told from the beginning by all my Boomer colleagues that the teacher pension was a good deal. With every year that passes, I can see they were not wrong. The deal I had has not been available to new teachers for some time. The same applies to retiring at 60 years old. I am sure I will not retire if I am in good health, but I will also be grateful for the income. I was also able to save a deposit across the late 1990s and early 2000s to buy a flat in outer London, then a house with my soon-to-be wife.

The reason I mention all of this is because, if necessary, I have assets to contribute to my own care in later life. Many of my generation, and increasingly large sections of the ones below, do not and see no prospects of gaining them. Unless government policy changes markedly and rapidly, the burden of this will fall on younger generations. The likelihood is that the resources will not be available to maintain health and social care, even the kind today's elderly have experienced. Quality of life in the autumn years may recede considerably.

There are other issues, including the ever-growing gap between rich and poor, and global peace and security, but I will avoid diving into too many rabbit holes at this stage.

The basic premise of this book is that Gen X does not understand Gen Z well enough, and a lot of problems can be solved if this changes. Ultimately, I would like to bridge the gap between generations and, in particular, between Gen X and Gen Z so the former understands the latter to a much greater extent than is currently the case.

It is possible for organisations to:

- recruit and retain the best of this generation
- develop them over time
- have a happy, motivated and highly engaged workforce, including their Gen Z staff
- ensure strong succession planning for middle and senior leadership
- make the most of the increasingly wide age gaps amongst their staff and use it as an asset.

It is possible for parents of those currently in their early to mid-twenties to:

- see the world through their eyes a little more clearly
- support them better.

There is a significant condition on all of this. The starting points for reflection and change must be with Gen X and not Gen Z. Too often I come across peers who expect Gen Z to fit into another generation's worldview, mindset and values without question. They expect them to have to go through the same experiences and want the same life.

I am not saying that all members of Gen Z are perfectly formed, nor that there is no need for change and reflection amongst them. I am saying that the change starts with us.

What to expect from *The Snowflake Myth*

This book is structured in three parts. The first focuses on the past, with some theory about generations and the key differences between them. Any theory about generations is a social construct; evolution has not moved so quickly that I am talking about different species. Having said that, across periods of time there are sufficient changes that mean the life experience of one group is different to what came before. That's what we'll cover in Part One.

In Part Two, I address the present and focus on a series of myths that collectively form The Snowflake Myth. I explain and counter the various myths and their roots in full, but also describe what I see as the key characteristics of Gen Z and the various approaches and strategies organisations and their leaders can use to address the issues. Although a key aim of the book is to demonstrate that the Snowflake perception is indisputably a myth, it is important to me to clarify what can be done to meet the needs of both generations. The principal focus of this book is to show what can be done well, rather than what is currently done badly.

The future is the focus of Part Three, and I approach this from three perspectives. The first is the future for Gen Z themselves as the eldest head into their thirties and beyond. Secondly, I talk about Gen Alpha who follow them and how they might be different to the generation immediately preceding them. The final perspective is about Gen X, and the legacy our generation could choose to leave if we so wished. For all their many attributes, there is an argument that Gen Z still needs us.

Although I will say throughout *The Snowflake Myth* that the level of disconnect between Generations X and Z is wider than it should be, the purpose of this book goes beyond bridging the gap. It is also about the future we can create together when that gap is bridged.

PART ONE

LEARNING FROM THE PAST

1

Generations: Who Belongs Where?

The concept of dividing time into periods for analytical purposes is not new. Time periods have been represented by different 'ages' (Stone, Bronze, Iron), monarchical dynasties (Normans, Tudors, Stuarts) or even dinosaurs (Triassic, Jurassic, Cretaceous). The length of each of those can vary considerably both within and across categories. Historians consider the Stone Age to be around 3 million years and the Iron Age a mere 700. The dinosaur ages range between 50 and 90 million years.[4]

Dinosaurs precede our *Homo sapiens* species, which has only been around for a few hundred thousand years. For most of that time, our existence has been as Thomas Hobbes described in *Leviathan*: 'No arts; no letters; no society; and which is worst of all, continual fear, and danger of violent death; and the life of man, solitary, poor, nasty, brutish, and short.'[5] Despite the differences between the generational

---

4   I don't know who is counting either.

5   Thomas Hobbes' *Leviathan* was the first book of political philosophy I ever read in the early '90s on my bachelor's degree course. It must have made an impression.

experiences I am about to describe, we have at least moved on since 1651.

The concept of a generation is not new either, but it is rarely established further than a period of years. It is defined as 'cohorts of people born in the same date range and who share similar cultural experiences'[6]. Typically, it has described family relationships and not broader social groupings. In 1863, the French lexicographer Emile Littré defined a generation as 'all people coexisting in society at any given time'.[xiii]

'Any given time' gives a lot of room for manoeuvre. On average, 1,700 people are born or die in the UK every day, between 600,000 and 700,000 over the course of a year. In 2023, three times as many immigrated to, or emigrated from, the UK. Across a nation pushing 70 million people, speaking hundreds of languages between them, where its inhabitants were born in every corner of the globe, it feels a stretch to claim 'similar cultural experiences'.

When this is taken a step further for the vast majority who have one or more social media accounts, each with an algorithm delivering bespoke content for every hour of the day its users are engaged, the idea that our experiences are 'similar' is even more far-fetched. It is not so long since the nation's choice of viewing and sources of 'content'[7] were far more restricted compared to today. This meant that audiences were larger. In this day and age, the likes of *Strictly Come Dancing* and *The Great British Bake Off* can still command an audience of many millions, but their peak figures are still less than half the 18.5 million who watched the Taylor vs Davis world snooker final

---

6   Karl Mannheim's *Essays on the Sociology of Knowledge*, published in 1952 .

7   I am having a Gen X dig here by putting it in inverted commas, but the use of the word 'content' in this sense is still relatively modern.

in the mid-'80s.[8] Even that is dwarfed by the 30 million, more than half of the UK population at the time, who watched the 1986 Christmas Day episode of *Eastenders*.

Beyond the few notable broadcast television successes of today lies a plethora of newer media forms such as podcasts where an exceptional audience might be hundreds of thousands within the UK. A TikTok video might hit millions of plays.[9] The drama offered by soap operas can now be found on social media. *Corrie* and *Eastenders* have staggered on, but with a fraction of their previous audiences. Consequently, the nation does not have the level of common experience as once was the case.

Technology has also enabled cultural experiences to be shared internationally. The most popular YouTube channels can have billions of views. Netflix, Apple and Amazon produce shows watched all around the world simultaneously. The same applies to our music, book and podcast consumption when our Spotify[10] listening habits are added to the mix.

---

8   That seemed bizarre even at the time. The fact that snooker was so popular is also an indication of the paucity of other sporting options available to watch. This match finished after midnight, and the nation stayed up to watch it. I didn't though, and 13-year-old me was quite cross about it. As for *Eastenders*, you might say Christmas Day viewing figures are out of context and that would be true. In that period of time, viewing figures of 18-20 million were typical. Before anyone says I am betraying my northern roots, I am aware that Eastenders viewing figures were regularly beaten by *Coronation Street* and *Emmerdale*.

9   A millisecond is all it takes to count, so not much of a play for many of them.

10   Other streaming platforms are available. I'm a Tidal person. I don't like playlists either, so there.

Even if our cultural life within the UK is far less homogenous than it was, we have more in common internationally than used to be the case. Dubbing major TV programmes into a variety of languages has only strengthened that. The same applies to the largest social media accounts. Over 10% of the world's population[11] follows Cristiano Ronaldo on social media. Two-thirds of them do so on Instagram, and they come from all over the world.

The generation question often applies to who might be the best singer, footballer or actor. Our shared global media experiences may mean there is less of a divergent view over who they are, as the statistics for viewing figures and social media accounts are freely available. Those statistics offer a perspective on who might be the best, given their popularity. It is a tenuous perspective,[12] but at least it indicates who the 'best' might be at any particular time.

Arguments over which icon defines a generation do not get us any closer to determining the length of 'a generation', nor understanding where to put the dividing lines between them. Let's tackle these in order.

The short answer is that both generation length and timeline are a social construct. When it comes to grouping human beings, a 'shift' from one generation to the next means that enough years have passed for circumstances to be noticeably different. A period of 15 years is

---

11   Almost 1 billion across all platforms, with a global population
      of 8 billion. I am sure there is some duplication here, but with
      approximately 650 million on Instagram at the time of writing, 'over
      10%' is a fair estimate.
12   The rabbit hole of 'most popular equalling the best' is one I am not
      going down, except to say common denominators are rarely a sign
      of true quality. Having said that, it does make AC/DC's 'Back in
      Black' the best rock album of the 1980s and I can live with that one.

enough to see sufficient economic, political, social and technological change to be worth analysing.

The case has been made to me that the pace of change in life means that 15 years is too long a period of time. It is certainly true that in terms of technology, as one example, what is available at the end of a generation may be very different to that at the start. Although that gap can clearly be seen between the start and end of Gen Z's years of birth, the same applies elsewhere.

It seems incredible now that there were only two years between the dawn of colour TV in the UK and the moon landings in 1969. You could argue that it is a false analysis, as the first colour picture was available decades before and mass travel to the moon seems as unlikely now as it did when Neil Armstrong first set foot on the lunar surface. Even so, it stands out as an example that technology moves quickly and not only in recent years.

It would be possible to analyse generations on the basis of the decade they were born, and therefore reduce the length by a third to 10 years. Doubtless this would help the idea sink deeper into the public consciousness, rather than have generations that do not start and finish with round numbers. It is feasible, although by its nature there would be more generations to analyse and less would have changed between them.

Alternatively, a generation could be determined to be two decades, a quarter of a century or any other number. A longer length of time would mean that more adults would be parents of the generation below instead of the increasingly common model of two generations apart, particularly the case for parents born in the second half of a generation.

In political post-war terms alone, 15 years is longer than both the Conservative governments of 1951 to 1964 and 2010 to 2024, and the Labour government of 1997 to 2010. It is also longer than Thatcher's term in office from 1979 to 1990, but not Major's time in charge after that until 1997. A generation is long enough for political change to be witnessed.

On the basis that it is sufficient time for any or all significant social, political, economic and sociological change, I am satisfied that 15 years is a viable period for generational analysis. In any case, I am not inventing sets of years myself, but using what has emerged as a broadly accepted set of dates by those who follow the topic. You will still find variations out there, but they do not undermine the broader concept.

It is worth adding that a generation as a concept is primarily western, by which I mean Western Europe, North America and Australasia. It also refers to the more affluent countries in global terms. Given this, it has limits. I am not claiming to analyse world events or global trends here. For the most part, the sources I use are from the UK (in whole or in part), some from USA and Canada, and various others from Western Europe. I have not explored how life has changed in the rest of the world. Primarily, this book focuses on the UK, and often England in particular. I am not saying that the whole of the western world has moved at the same pace, although on the surface there is much in common.

The 'affluent' element matters because economic and financial factors drive changes to happen at similar times. Political leaders will change when elections happen, and often in between. The speed at which social and technological changes make their way through the populace will vary.

I have seen other dates used for generations elsewhere, particularly for Gen Z. The start date for Gen Z varies between the mid-to-late 1990s and the end a little either side of 2010. Had I worked with 1995 as the beginning of Gen Z, there would have been a professional convenience for me while writing this book, as I first took up post as a headteacher in 2006. This would make the first set of 11-year-olds I worked with in that role the first Gen Z arriving at secondary school.

Given that a generation is a social construct, there is no right or wrong answer to when one starts and ends. However, ahead of giving a talk, I noticed companies' HR leads sending me generational breakdown figures of their workforce based on the same dates, so I decided to fall in line.

Whatever the ranges I have seen for Gen Z, the key event of the Global Financial Crisis (GFC) took place within it, followed by years of austerity that affected their young lives. The 'dividing lines' between generations are neither a hard stop nor a guillotine. A little haziness is actually helpful in this respect. The end points do not need to be marked by seismic events. It is what happens in between those end points that matters.

Naming and dating the generations

Despite the fact that the concept in its modern sense was first used in the nineteenth century, generations were not widely used until the mid-to-late twentieth century. The first recorded use of the phrase 'Baby Boomer' was in 1963 just as the last of that generation was born. It is at least the easiest one to work out the origins of its name.

The Silent Generation is named for the time when supposedly 'children were seen but not heard'. Generation X was so called because, allegedly, it did not wish to be defined. Millennials are sometimes referred to as Generation Y due to the alphabetical convenience that would become a trend. The idea of a Millennial was that the oldest would 'come of age' around the time of the new millennium.[13] Given this, the idea of a whole 15-year generation called Millennials presents as a contradiction in terms. It is the most common name, so I will stick to it here. Generation Z followed and the alphabetical sequence resumes, old-money car-registration style, to A or Alpha.

'Gen' is now commonly used interchangeably with 'Generation' and the same will apply in this book.

I will emphasise strongly that with Gen Z, or any other generation come to that, I am not talking about a homogenous group. The generation you 'belong' to does not feature on your birth certificate or passport. If it needs to be repeated, all generations belong to the same species. The differences within any generation (intra-generational) will always be more significant than across generations (inter-generational). I would strongly recommend everyone is treated as an individual in any workplace.

The concept of generations is intended to analyse the impact of some common experiences and not to stereotype personalities. Although my experience is that Gen Z is interested in how the hand they have been dealt compares to previous generations, more than any other generation, they are deeply uninterested in being neatly defined as a whole.

---

13   What 'come of age' means is in itself generational. A more typical answer these days is 18 (or earlier), but it used to be 21.

	YEARS OF BIRTH
Silent Generation	1925–1945
Baby Boomers	1946–1964
Generation X	1965–1980
Millenials	1981–1996
Generation Z	1997–2012
Generation Alpha	2013–2028

Figure 1: Table of generations by year

Analysing the overlaps

Let's explore the idea that there is not a guillotine between different generations a little further. For example, if a sibling group of three was born within a five-year period across the late '70s and early '80s then, technically, they would be split between Gen X and Millennials. Given the five-year range between eldest and youngest, their childhood experience would have much in common, although it is likely that by the time the youngest sibling had finished their formative years, there would be some new toys or technology that made their experience stand out.

It is a moot point as to whether people would rather be the eldest of one generation or the youngest of another. I am the father of a daughter born in 2011, and this discussion has come up at home when I was pondering which set of generational dates to settle upon. She told me that she was 'definitely a Gen Z and not an Alpha because the Alphas are really annoying'.[14]

Although it is helpful as a means of analysing trends over time, the concept of a generation does have its limits. Fifteen years may be

---

14   And so it begins...

enough time for political, social and economic changes, but plenty of change happens within that period too. The pandemic and immediate post-pandemic years are a good example of when life changed markedly and unexpectedly for very large groups of people within a very short time period.

At the time of writing, approximately half of Gen Z is currently in the workplace and the other half is of an age to be in full-time education. In this book, I am focusing primarily on the older half of Gen Z, currently in their twenties. A full analysis of the generation in the workplace will only be possible in the future.

For the most part, I am going to avoid using hybrid terms such as Xennial (born around the Gen X/Millennial boundary) or Zillennial (Millennial/Gen Z boundary), partly to keep it simple. It is not that I am wedded to the idea that a 15-year period is the only viable model, but I would also like to offer you some consistency.

That consistency is important not least because there has been a tendency for the media to conflate generations. I have seen a series of examples where 'Millennials' and 'Gen Z' are used interchangeably or collectively. Millennials also went through a period of various unkind descriptions in the past. The idea that there is a younger generation in the workplace already seems to have come as a surprise.

This conflation might be restricted to those who still buy and read newspapers for whom the definition of 'young people today' might be a lot broader. Either way, I will seek to avoid this conflation. Having said that, I will draw upon my experience of teaching and working with Millennials over the course of the book. Although there are significant differences between the formative years of both generations, the trends that Gen Z are experiencing did not begin the moment the oldest members of the generation reached the workplace.

Differences across generations

Events shape generations, although they may not form the dividing line between them. The Boomer generation began after the end of the Second World War as the troops came home, but it is not always so straightforward, particularly now that 15 years has become the standard length of a generation.

This book focuses on Gen Z rather than the experiences of every twentieth-century or post-war generation. The table below is my attempt to condense decades of history in order to show some of the key changes over time.

This list contains a few of the main events that affected each generation. It is a small selection and does not always have a direct equivalent in each corner. My view, from the perspective of someone who taught a little history, is that the hardest history skill to learn is chronology. Knowing about a set of events is one thing, but remembering or working out how or why they came in a particular order is something else.

For the purpose of this book, the key part is the impact an event had on a generation, rather than it falling within the years of birth. This is not to say that 9/11 or social media only affected Millennials, but that it had the most impact for them. Often it is because of their age at the time and the impact on their education and early professional life. These are not always easy arguments to make and are frequently tenuous.

BABY BOOMER	GENERATION X
Post-WW2	End of Cold War
Moon landing	Big Bang
Swinging '60s	Dial-up internet
First TV	Handful of TV channels
Mass media develops	Workaholics
Civil rights	Latchkey kids
MILLENNIAL	**GENERATION Z**
9/11	Global Financial Crisis
Globalisation	Automation
Social media	Broadband/streaming
Internet emergence	Gig/sharing economy
Multiple TV channels	Internet commercialised
Work smarter	TV apps/YouTube

Figure 2: Key events for each generation

If I explore the differences between Millennials and Gen Z as a direct comparison, it looks something like this:

MILLENIALS/GEN Y	GEN Z
Boomer/Gen X parents	Gen X/Millenial parents
Digitally connected	Digital natives
Netflix	YouTube
Economic prosperity	Austerity
Experiences shared in person	Some friends will never meet
Selfies	Multiple online identities
'Me' generation	'We' generation

Figure 3: Millennials vs Gen Z

There is plenty to debate here, and there would be members of each generation who can see themselves in other elements. It is a set of deliberate generalisations to make a point. It is likely that those closer to the cusp will identify more strongly with aspects of earlier or later generations. In other words, the closer to the invisible line between generations you are, the more you may be shaped by cultural events that don't impact your generational peers towards the middle of the generation period.

I will go through a few examples to make the point and explain some terms along the way.

The concept of 'latchkey kids' originated as the percentage of women in the workplace increased significantly.[15] Consequently, as both parents went out to work, their children let themselves in after school. Clearly, that practice is not restricted to Gen X and is likely to have tailed off as working from home, or other flexible arrangements, has become more popular.

From one perspective, YouTube is older than Netflix, despite the fact I have put it under Gen Z rather than the older Millennials. YouTube began in 2005, and Netflix[16] launched its streaming service in 2007. The reason YouTube is in the Gen Z column is because of the explosion of popularity of the platform, including amongst its younger audience who use the YouTube platform as one of many TV apps. They are also accustomed to shorter videos, compared to 'boxset bingeing' of Netflix.

A 'digital native' is applied to Gen Z as they have not known a time before broadband, smartphones, social media and so on. They did

---

15   It was an increase of approximately a third from 1955 (46%) to 1985 (61%).

16   For the record, Netflix started in 1997 as a DVD rental service.

not grow up in an analogue world which then became connected digitally. A lot of younger Millennials would also identify with this experience.

These days, the phrase 'Big Bang' might be more likely to be applied to the origins of the universe and would therefore be more relevant to the dinosaur references earlier in the chapter.[17] Instead, I am referring to a range of measures implemented simultaneously in the UK Stock Exchange in 1986.[18] This is a good example of a phrase that meant one thing, shifted to something else, then finally went back to the original.

In short, there are a lot of grey areas to consider and there is not a universal opinion about where dividing lines are drawn. Consequently, people from one generation will identify with the other trends. The chronological order of events is not in dispute, just the lines between them.

Trends in the newest workforce generation

The size of the Gen Z population, including those old enough to work, is often larger than perceived. The 2021 census showed roughly even numbers between Boomers, Gen X, Millennials and Gen Z of 13 to 14 million.

In 2025, Gen Z will represent over a quarter of the UK workforce and there will be more of them than Boomers. This is despite the

---

17   Give or take 13.5 billion years.

18   The most visual element of the changes was that trading moved from the bustling stock market floor to screens, but it was accompanied by a stack of deregulatory measures. There is a case that these changes laid the foundations for the GFC two decades later, but that's a topic for another book.

fact that the percentage of those over 65 years old who are in the workforce has risen from 4.6% in 2001 to 11.2% in 2023.[xiv] The cost of living crisis may have led to some returning to the workforce, but the trend started long before. Delayed retirements, often driven by an increase in the state pension age and the reduction in workplace pensions, have been a feature for some time too. By 2030, Gen Z will represent over a third of the global workforce. There may be more Millennials and Gen X in the workforce at present, and a much higher proportion of them are in management positions, but with every passing year that will close until the early 2030s.

Those figures are all very well, but why do they matter? The brief answer to that question below will form the core argument of the rest of this book. In Part Two, I explore the underlying themes specifically.

Gen Z is the most important generational shift so far, but their experiences and outlook are not understood well enough by those who have come before them. As already mentioned, Gen Z has huge, as yet mostly untapped, potential to meet the challenges of today. Some of these challenges are most relevant to them, including the poor financial situation they have inherited. Others affect us all, including the climate crisis, the divide between rich and poor and an ageing population.

The oldest of the generation are already making their mark, whether within established organisations or in setting up their own. The challenges faced by organisations in recruiting and retaining the best have been made harder by failing to come up with solutions to a falling birth rate from the mid-1990s to early 2000s and by not competing with the appeal of Gen Z setting up their own enterprises.

The Gen Z members who are in, or about to join, the workforce have experienced more difficult economic times, a greater level of uncertainty and an upbringing with technology that was more powerful and dangerous than their parents and teachers truly understood. All of this has significant implications for them in the workplace and their adult lives.

While the challenges are considerable, there are also significant opportunities for Gen Z and those who work with them.

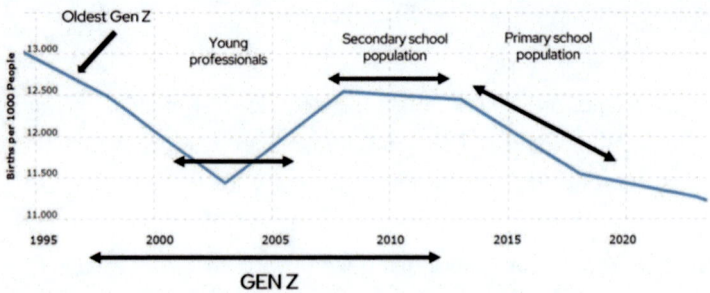

Figure 4: UK birth rates 1995 to 2024[19]

Some of the issues lie in the demographics. Part of the reason it has become harder to recruit and retain Gen Z is because there have been fewer of them coming into the workplace. Birth rates dropped from the mid-'90s to the early 2000s. This has caused a particular issue in secondary schools, as one example, as the birth rate for the second half of Gen Z went back up to levels at the start.

There has been a perfect storm of more teenagers to educate at the same time that the number of young professionals has declined.

_____

19   Of course, as the years pass the groups who represent the 'current' primary school pupils or young professionals will change, but the continuous fall from 2008 will have a significant impact on how pensions and adult social care (amongst others) are funded.

The rise in birth rates for those born in the latter half of the noughties does not quite mean that the 'cavalry is coming', but it should make a difference. More young professionals will be available to recruit.

New technology has also amplified the deficit of young professionals. I remember delivering many assemblies on a general careers theme where I told students they would be doing jobs in the future that had not been invented yet. It feels more than a little odd years down the line to be doing one myself.[20]

What difference has new technology made? There are several answers to that question.

Jobs have been created, partly through the hyper-niching and specialisation of work. If I take one area of my work as an example, the number of leadership coaches[21] is estimated to have doubled from 2019 to 2024 to approximately 150,000.[xv] For some, it will be a string to their bow in an existing role; for others, a new job opportunity; for many, their own business. The qualification will only go so far if you do not specialise.[22] Saying that you 'can coach anyone' is too generic in this day and age. You need to stand out from the crowd. If instead you choose to be a coach for 'knackered mid-life women in the public sector'[23], and you market

---

20 While leadership coaching, team coaching, training, public speaking and writing books have existed in one form or another for many years, the 'jobs that had not been invented' are not just jobs in new areas like artificial intelligence, but the increased ability to monetise activities and to do so online.

21 Leadership or executive coaching rather than sports coaches.

22 I feel Sarah Short on my shoulder telling me to say that 82% of coaching businesses do not survive, and the ones who do have an established niche.

23 For this, see Sarah Clein at https://sarahclein.co.uk/.

effectively for that specific audience, you can find your potential clients.

Technology has now made it possible to provide a service for people who really need it but previously had no chance of finding it or knowing it could even exist. Businesses can create their own audience on social media, design a simple website optimised to rank on search engines, then create content tailored to their ideal client so potential customers can find out about and buy the service. In effect, this has created a lot of jobs that previously did not exist. Technology has facilitated the ultimate division of labour.

The portfolio career is now a reality for many thousands. By a portfolio, I mean a range of activities, some of which might involve existing on a payroll and others on a freelance basis. Portfolio careers can take many shapes, from two to many activities, from part-time to full-time or chunks of time in and out of work. It enables individuals to start an activity, which may one day be the 'main gig', and build it up over time, or to play a role in someone else's side hustle. While there is a lot of this among Gen Zers, there is also plenty amongst Boomers too who are the generation most likely to hold two jobs[xvi].

Barriers to entry of starting your own one-person internet-based business, as an increasingly common model, are very low. Bricks-and-mortar businesses carry comparatively significant costs, which most internet businesses do not need to bear in order to be successful.

All of this was accelerated by the pandemic as we were stuck at home during the Covid-19 lockdowns and worked out that meaningful activity could be carried out by virtual meetings. The pandemic also came as the oldest cohorts of Gen Z hit their early twenties. The need to be resourceful, look elsewhere and, in some cases, maintain a way of working that suited them drove a lot of risk-taking and innovation, which otherwise would not have taken place. One legacy of Covid was the possibilities that every generation saw for their personal world of work.

When the whole generation hits the workplace...

Approximately half of Gen Z is still in school or other full-time education. They have yet to reach the workplace and much could happen before the final ones do in the early 2030s. There is a long time to go before we can make a full evaluation. In Part Three, I explore what the future might look like; it is necessarily speculative. Economic circumstances, as one example, may have changed a great deal before the youngest of Gen Z reach the workplace, by which time the oldest will be approaching 40. I have written this book based on my experience and the evidence to date, but that evidence base is ever-growing.

One clarification must be made here, which is that generational analysis must not conflate the experience of a cohort over the course of their life with what it is like to live in a particular stage. The experiences of those who are 20 and those who are 40 will vary because responsibilities tend to be greater for the latter at home and work. I am not saying that Gen Z's values and outlook will stay the same from now on either but do argue that those formative experiences carry a legacy.

This book focuses on how Gen Z's formative years have been different from that of older generations, and the impact their experience has had. I want to separate what might be generic life-stage experiences applicable to all generations and what I see as being specific to Gen Z. At the same time, I will cover some of those generic experiences too. Gen Z is not the first generation to struggle.

Endnotes

i   Saunt, R. (2023, April 21). More than HALF of managers have been forced to fire Gen Z workers. *Mail Online*. https://www.dailymail.co.uk/femail/article-11996253/More-HALF-managers-forced-fire-Gen-Z-workers.html

ii   Coulter, C. (2021, November 1). Gen-Z workers are terrifying their millennial bosses with woke demands. *Mail Online*. https://www.dailymail.co.uk/news/article-10149905/Gen-Z-workers-terrifying-millennial-bosses-woke-demands.html

iii   Collins, T. (2019, May 15). Millennials and Gen Z really ARE snowflakes. *Mail Online*. https://www.dailymail.co.uk/sciencetech/article-7033111/Millennials-Gen-Z-really-snowflakes.html

iv   Harding, E. (2022, January 1). Rise of social media has "turned university students into snowflakes." *Mail Online*. https://www.dailymail.co.uk/news/article-10359887/Rise-social-media-turned-university-students-snowflakes.html

v   *Vitality health and life insurance.* (n.d.-e). Vitality Health and Life Insurance. https://www.vitality.co.uk/media/poor-health-at-work-is-responsible-for-138bn-loss-to-uk-economy-each-year

vi   Hamilton, J. (2024c, November 1). Gen Z and millennials are missing one day of work per week due to this reason. *Metro*. https://metro.co.uk/2024/11/01/gen-z-millennials-missing-one-day-work-per-week-due-this-reason-21902423/

vii   *50% of Gen Z workers think about j – HRZone.* (2023c, December 30). HRZone. https://hrzone.com/blog/50-of-gen-z-workers-think-about-leaving-their-job/#:~:text=Employees%20were%20asked%20if%20they,25%2D39

viii   Pardo, S. B., & Pardo, S. B. (2024, January 22). Number of Gen Z directors jumps 42% in a year – there are now 243,000 young people running businesses. *International Accounting Bulletin*. https://www.internationalaccountingbulletin.com/news/number-of-gen-z-directors-jumps-42-in-a-year-there-are-now-243000-young-people-running-businesses/

ix   Chan, C. (2024, June 13) *2024 Hiring Trends Survey: What Makes a Great Job Candidate?*, Resume Genius. https://resumegenius.com/

blog/job-hunting/hiring-trends-survey

x Dickinson, C. (2024b, November 6). *Impellus | Why Gen Z are saying no to middle management*. Impellus. https://impellus.com/articles/high-stress-low-reward-why-gen-z-are-saying-no-to-middle-management/

xi Smith, M. (2022, September 8). *Quiet quitting: how hard do Britons say they're working?* YouGov. https://yougov.co.uk/economy/articles/43705-quiet-quitting-how-hard-do-britons-say-theyre-work

xii Bruce, J. (2023, August 8). *3 Things Gen Z teaches us about Quiet quitting*. Forbes. https://www.forbes.com/sites/janbruce/2023/08/08/3-things-gen-z-teaches-us-about-quiet-quitting/

xiii En, É. L. ;. F. G. (n.d.). *Dictionnaire Littré – Dictionnaire de la langue française*. https://www.littre.org/

xiv *Employment rate 65 + People: % – Office for National Statistics*. (2025, February 18). https://www.ons.gov.uk/employmentandlabourmarket/peopleinwork/employmentandemployeetypes/timeseries/lfk6/lms

xv *Coaching Industry Report – Insights, Trends and Statistics*. (n.d.). https://www.robinwaite.com/coaching-industry-report

xvi Grewal, H.K. (2014, October 1). *Boomers more likely than Gen Z to hold two jobs*. Facilitate Magazine. https://www.facilitatemagazine.com/content/news/2024/10/01/boomers-more-likely-hold-two-jobs-gen-z

2

Every Generation Faces the Same Issues

Contending with serious and potentially cataclysmic global issues is not a problem reserved for Gen Z. Younger Boomers faced what seemed to be the very real possibility of 'the world being blown up'[1] in the early '60s as the Cold War and its proliferation of nuclear weapons developed at pace. Looking back at the Cuban Missile Crisis with modern eyes seems particularly terrifying, not least because the minute-by-minute news we now expect was not available by social media.

The truth is many of the issues that face Gen Z as they enter the workforce are things we've all been through. In this chapter, I will explore the parallels between the generations' experiences.

---

[1]   This is embarrassing so I am keeping it to a footnote. No one explained to me what 'blowing up the world' meant as a child so I took it pretty literally. My recollection is of incredibly large craters from nuclear explosions at best to an Earth which was barely spherical. Was I alone in this?

The threat of nuclear war was not restricted to the early 1960s. The arms race of the '80s was another existential threat as the two superpowers of the USA and the USSR[2] battled their way to the largest stockpile of both weaponry and allies. It is easy to forget how powerful and dangerous the USSR was seen to be decades ago, and that the mere 500 miles between Britain's borders and the Iron Curtain felt very short.

In the 2020s, there have already been two particularly high-profile conflicts in Gaza and Ukraine.[3] Modern technology provides video footage and on-demand updates if you choose to engage with them. The scale of death and destruction has felt unimaginable and prolonged. It is hard to believe that the numbers killed by war were far smaller in the first quarter of the twenty-first century than the final quarter of the twentieth.[4]

Climate change is a further existential threat, albeit one that is happening gradually and unpredictably with increasing evidence that the impact is irreversible and well underway. The numbers who have died as a result of it so far are far less than those who have died from famine and disease. I understand this is not comparing like with

---

2   The former Soviet Union dissolved into its 15 constituent republics in the early 1990s. Even though modern events show what Russia is capable of doing, it is not considered to be a 'superpower' in the same breath in the USA as was the case.

3   This is in addition to ongoing conflicts in Myanmar, which accounted for 20,000 deaths in 2024, and several across Africa (including Ethiopia and Sudan) which accounted for almost 50,000.

4   Getting precise figures on this is not straightforward. Very approximately, almost 20 million died in war in the last quarter of the twentieth century, compared to less than 3.5 million in the first quarter of the twenty-first.

like[5] and do not wish to underestimate the imminent and significant nature of the catastrophe. I would say that there was a time when it looked like the issues regularly reported on in the '80s and '90s would never progress either, and the scale of tragedy was high.[6]

The cost of housing is a significant issue today, and with good reason. The price of rent in itself prohibits young professionals from being able to save, let alone the rest of the cost of living. The cost of borrowing is very different today compared to that experienced by those Boomers and older Gen X who had mortgages in the early '90s. The interest rate hikes of the early '90s left many not only without their homes, but a collapse in prices also left them in negative equity. The rise to 15% meant the end of home ownership for some, and either a delay in returning to ownership and/or in paying off the debts accrued through negative equity. Deposits may have been much cheaper than by modern standards, but the cost of borrowing could be volatile as well as high. Throughout the 2010s, the average mortgage rate for those on variable deals was 2.84%[7] and the Bank of England base rate was 0.5%.

On top of that, many took out endowment mortgages, which did not turn out to be the incredible deal that was advertised.[8] The result was that families found themselves borrowing additional funds rather than enjoying the bonuses over time.

---

5   The impact of climate change also has a significant impact on food supply, and therefore famine and disease as well.

6   I do not want to give the impression that the number of deaths by famine and disease is declining inevitably either.

7   Office of National Statistics.

8   A form of interest-only mortgage, where a separate sum was paid into a life-assurance policy. The idea was that when the mortgage was paid off, the policy holder would receive an additional sum. Many did not and found themselves with additional debts to pay. They are not in common use now.

As housing is the largest cost of any household, high interest rates also had a significant impact on the financial independence of those who suffered. The rise in interest rates and collapse in property prices was, unsurprisingly, accompanied by an economic recession in the early '90s.

Second-generation snowflakes

The Snowflake Myth did not start with Gen Z either. Although I do not remember being called that name specifically, I do remember the accusation being laid at both me and my peers that we were 'soft'. I have strong memories of being told that as I had been born some years after the war, and also after the end of rationing, I had no idea of what life could really be like and how lucky I was. The end of corporal punishment in schools in 1986[9] was considered to be a particularly unfair move from those who had endured it in their own childhoods, and it also left them as parents (and, in some cases, teachers[10]) without the one sanction they imagined they could rely upon to work. 'That cane used to rule England' is what I was regularly told by those 20 years older than me, often accompanied by words to the effect of 'you young folks don't know you are born these days'.

Beyond that, there were changes in the workplace and working practices. The post-war period saw a significant decline in both primary and secondary production. The decline in the latter was

---

9   It took another 17 years for this to spread to all private schools in the UK.

10   I was once part of a group threatened with the cane by a teacher who said he had permission from the headteacher to use it. We knew he hadn't, yet the fact he was white with fury and had it out of the cupboard ready to go made us think it might happen anyway. When he hadn't been kept up all night by his baby son (as was the case on that occasion), he was a decent guy. I won't name him, but buy me a pint of IPA and I will give you the full reenactment.

accelerated by the policies of the Thatcher government across the 1980s. Growing up in a coal mining town, with pits all around us, made me particularly aware of this, including during the miners' strike of 1984-85. Although I did not go to school with miners' kids or live next door to miners, it was impossible not to feel the strike going on around you. I remember seeing the endless line of coaches holding all the police on their way to Orgreave, the most violent flashpoint of the strike. Administrative or clerical jobs were often seen as the soft option.

I remember an incident while playing cricket in my teens with a men's team. I was in the outfield and failed to prevent the ball going over the boundary rope. "What do you do for work, lad? Do you work in a bank or something?" The word 'bank' was spat out in pure disgust as though he could think of no lower form of labour. In effect, I was being called a snowflake there and then.

Those who had endured life in the mine often did not consider sitting at a desk and 'pen-pushing' (also said in disgust) to be proper work. Regularly working 9 to 5 rather than night shifts, weekends or other anti-social arrangements was also seen as a relative luxury. There were plenty who had to rotate their shifts, so they would spend one week working during the hours they had been trying to sleep the previous week.

'Kids these days have no idea, do they?' was a common theme throughout my childhood. Colour television, electricity in every room and a full set of white goods were also aspects I was regularly told I should not take for granted because 'I wouldn't survive without them'.

This is a gut feeling rather than an evidence-based conclusion, but the gap between the formative years of the Boomers born soon after the end of World War 2 and the older half of Gen X feels at least as marked as that between the latter and the first half of Gen Z. The gap between parents who typically experienced rationing, leaving school at 15 (or earlier) and risky manual work with worse working conditions than would be tolerated today and a generation who were educated for longer, had more alternatives to manual labour and only saw ration books in museums was considerable.

I can remember my mum saying that she had a fear that the day would come when I would have to fight as her father had. He was an Army captain at 21 in what used to be called Burma (now Myanmar) and brought home memories he would never discuss. I am quite sure that even if I had to go to war, his sage advice would not have been of much use to me. There are many walks of life in which I would have been wholly useless, and the military is one of them. For me, it was never a real consideration.

It is also true that the older generations had less experience of life before parenthood, as they were younger when they had children than tends to be the case now. My mum was barely 24 when she had me as her first child, and she was a few months older than the average for a new mother at the time. The average age for a mother giving birth for the first time is over 30 today[11]. As a proportion of an entire lifetime, it may not be huge, but in terms of adult life, today's new mother has twice as much life experience.

All of that makes a big difference in parents having wisdom to pass on to their child. While I accept the pace of change in life today feels significant, I do not agree that it is on the scale of the paradigm shift that came before.

Gen Z is also not the first generation to have to adapt quickly to new technology, or face the prospect of it threatening jobs, livelihoods or work-life balance. The speed and convenience of email was thought

---

11   In 1972 it was 23.8, in 2024 30.9.

to be a giant time-saver in the beginning, while also putting thousands of Royal Mail workers at risk. It did seem a much better way of doing things than the physical in-trays, wire baskets or pigeon holes. The modern horrors of the endless 'reply all' conversation, pestering by your boss (and everyone else) at all hours or receiving a long series of delay delivery emails at 8:00 every morning[12] to ruin your day did not exist. The same applies to working out whether the message thread that requires your apparent immediate attention was on email, Slack, Teams, WhatsApp or any other platform designed to increase productivity.

The first nine years of my career went by without me ever sending an email. Arriving as a deputy headteacher at the school I would later go on to lead, I remember thinking 'this place is seriously cutting edge' when a teacher told me they had sent me an email.

That comment in itself is revealing. There was a period of time when we were not so welded to our PCs and laptops, and therefore also our inboxes. Those who used emails might have to physically notify those who didn't. Laptops lacked the memory and processing speed of today, and were less popular. Our use of computers was also not a mobile experience, and the proliferation of coffee shops and co-working spaces was yet to take place. Internet cafes proliferated for a while. The coffee shops that existed did not have conveniently located plug sockets. Furthermore, as smartphones were not the standard, email was not portable.

The way in which artificial intelligence is described as a problem to the economic wellbeing of many reminds me of how the internet was first talked about. I remember being told that it was a bad decision to become a teacher because there would be no need for schools in the internet age. The phrase 'information superhighway' provoked both

---

12   Guilty on this one. I used to do a lot of this until someone finally told me that they dread the '8:00 am moment'.

intrigue and alarm in equal measures. It was not just schools that were due to be redundant, but bookshops, libraries and newsagents.[13] All manufacturing processes would become automated as robots would 'take over the world'.

In the end, few realised that new technology would create jobs that could not previously exist, and millions of them. The same applies now to artificial intelligence.

Boomers also experienced the first meaningful wave of computerisation. A crowd gathering around a cashpoint these days might indicate criminal activity, but back in the day it was the awe and wonder of watching money appear out of the wall. The automation of any task was considered a threat to jobs, and potentially civilisation as we know it. We looked at the BBC computers at school with a sense of reverence, along with the 'ICT lab' that housed them.

Social changes for Gen Z

Gen Z's propensity for social justice and using its voice to achieve it also has its forebears. Boomers led the way in the civil rights and anti-war movements of the '60s and '70s. Both Boomers and Gen X populated the Campaign for Nuclear Disarmament marches and Greenham Common, although it was the older half of the latter who led the way in the Poll Tax riots. We may remember the large scale of the marches against the Second Iraq War, but the scepticism about the need for the first one in the early 1990s after the invasion of Kuwait was also accompanied by protests and marches on the streets.[14] It was not just miners who took industrial action in the 1970s

---

13   The newsagent prediction was not quite true, but there has been a
        sea change. The word has effectively disappeared from our lexicon.
14   In London alone, the size of the protest was estimated at 100,000
        with further protests across a number of cities in the UK.

and 1980s, and the legislation of the day did not make strikes as difficult to organise as is now the case.

Turning to relationships, the dazzling range of dating apps and platforms may make it easy to get a date, but they are no guarantee of a meaningful connection emerging. Those from older generations had their own dating issues too. My parents met when my mum was 18 and my dad was 24. Three years later they were married, and I arrived three years after that. In order to live together, the social norm was that you had to be married. If there was a pregnancy, then a swift marriage was the basic expectation to avoid 'shame being brought on the family'. Divorce could bring the same; as that social norm receded, divorce rates rose sharply[15], as did the number of single parents.

Gen Z faces problems with the unstable and unprotected world of the gig economy, but is not the first to have to deal with problematic working conditions. While the 'job for life' described by Boomers had much to commend it for a post-war generation rebuilding the country, it did not suit everyone. A steady, reliable, reasonably well-paid job may have been a valuable asset to build a life around, but it did not always fit the strengths of those who had them. To change career, or even to contemplate it, was a risk too far for many, regardless of the level of job satisfaction. Those who ended up in work that did not suit them were more likely to put up and shut up.

Boomers and older Gen X increasingly became subject to takeovers, asset-stripping, restructures or downsizing. The flexibility of moving from job to job, and potentially career to career, and location to

---

15   The 1969 Divorce Reform Act was a key catalyst, but it clearly reflected demand. Within a few years, the annual number of divorces (in England and Wales) tripled from 40,000 to 120,000. Twenty years later, it had risen by a further third.

location too, had its advantages, but not all of it was voluntary. Unemployment, and particularly 'mass' unemployment, did not feature in the news until we reached the previously unimaginable total of 1 million unemployed in 1978. The famous 'Labour isn't working' campaign, which played a part in the Conservatives' general election win of 1979, was seen in a different light as unemployment moved to 2 million and then 3 million in the 1980s.

Equality

'Work-life balance' was not a phrase in common use amongst Boomers.[16] To be a 'workaholic' could be a badge of honour, at least as much as it might be considered a problem. It was less normal to bring work home than it is today for the simple reason it was impractical. As the alternative to the desk was not available, people did one or more of arriving early, staying late or returning at the weekend.

The clearer separation between work and home did not necessarily lead to a healthy balance between the two. The same applied to relationships between men and women where the former was conventionally expected to be the breadwinner and the latter the housekeeper.

The idea of challenging your boss about working practices, or stating that you were not coming into work because of a mental health issue, was only slightly more tenable for Gen X than it was for Boomers. The demands of having both parents working, and needing to work to cover the mortgage they had taken out, also had practical implications for childcare and therefore work-life balance.

---

16   It is not always easy to pin these things down. As the percentage of women in the workplace grew, arrangements for part-time working and maternity leave grew with it.

Gen Z is far less likely to face issues about whether women should be working or not, whether mental health is the 'equivalent' of physical health or an expectation that working all hours is the expected culture. However, too many have experienced having to work at home when they would rather be in a physical workplace, gig economy wages and the reality of 'living at work' rather than 'working from home'. The additional flexibility available to so many has not led to an increase in happiness or life satisfaction, as is described in Chapter 4.

Vocalising concerns about mental health did not start with Gen Z, although in retrospect this was not always obvious. Those who drank to excess night after night, or developed other addictions to nicotine, marijuana and stronger alternatives, did not often feel they were doing so out of choice. It was not the done thing to talk about, or draw attention to, feelings and emotions. Many Boomers experienced their parents, perhaps particularly their fathers, not wanting to open up about anything, despite their inner turmoil. The recognition and resources for mental health were limited at best, including for those who had experienced the horrors of war.

Awareness increased for Gen X, but it took some time for mental health to be seen as a health issue of the same status as physical health. Decades passed until the stigma started to recede and for an open discussion to take place. This has been too late for far too many. Those who suffered from depression had to fight hard for it to be taken seriously, including amongst employers. Counselling and therapy were often considered to be the preserve of the middle classes who had 'less to complain about'.

The culture of openly sharing thoughts and feelings in the formative years of social media did lead to positive outcomes for many Millennials. The ability for others to comment on posts clearly had its downsides, but within private Facebook groups or internet forums people could have their mental health concerns supported and validated by others. The stigma around engaging was, slowly, replaced by an encouragement to do so.

Gen Z may have inherited a world where mental health does not have that stigma, and where any and every issue can be shared in public and at length. If anything, the stigma is now not sharing openly. If I had known that this would become the culture in the 2020s, I would have assumed that this would mean a severe reduction in the numbers who required support with their mental health. The unfortunate truth, as described in Chapter 4, could not be more different. We have a mental health epidemic amongst Gen Z in this country, and resources to counter it are limited at best.

Older generations have often been in the shoes of our younger counterparts even in a different context. Gen X's amnesia can feel convenient too often. It was not so long ago that we faced our own unique challenges and held frustrations that our parents' generation either did not 'get it' or try to do so. The exercise now is to develop empathy and understanding for today's young people and break the cycle of intergenerational disconnect. Gen X's relationships with Gen Z are established whether at work or in the family. We have a responsibility to understand them better than at present.

PART TWO

TODAY'S GEN Z MYTHS AND MISUNDERSTANDINGS

3

The Myth of Lazy

When I was in my early twenties and at university, some of my peers decided the only 'morning' hours they would see were the small ones. Getting out of bed at 2:00 pm, missing their lectures and tutorials along the way, was perfectly acceptable. Decades later, when those same peers complained about their young colleagues arriving late for work, I did not offer much empathy.

Laziness is the first stereotype I heard about Gen Z that really annoyed me. And it's a myth. The idea of laziness among this cohort is the most dissonant from my own experience.

In this chapter, I'm going to uncover why we have this misperception and demonstrate how Gen Z are, in my opinion, an incredibly diligent generation.

Workplace observations

When I hear Gen X and the media talk about laziness among the youngest workplace generation, here's what they say.

Gen Z is lazy because:

- "They leave on the dot every day! They just do not know what it takes for this business to succeed, or what they have to do to get somewhere in life. When I was their age, working late, evenings and weekends was just how it was and we had to get on with it. The number of working hours used not to mean anything, now it is seen as a limit."
- "If it is not in their job description, they do not want to do it. They say 'why should I have to?' It is as though this is the first time they have ever had a job."
- "If I ever ask them to do something they have never done before, they stare at me blankly and mutter a few objections before they say, 'No, I can't do that'. They are reluctant to get involved in any form of problem-solving at all. Looking at the first page of Google hits or a two-minute YouTube video is as far as they want to get."
- "When I send them an urgent email after hours, I get nothing back. I don't do it often, but for them the end of the working day is just a hard stop. The following day I am told it will happen when they get to work, but not before. I've had people leave the building while I'm still talking to them before."
- "There's one thing I just don't get. I know the cost of living is hard for them, rent is expensive and they don't expect to be able to buy a place to live. So, why do they not go for the promotions when they become available? They need more money and it's sitting there for them, but they aren't interested. They would rather stay where they are than put the effort in."
- "They do not put in the effort to travel to work! I need them in the office so I can see what they are doing and be on hand to help. But the time to commute is too much of an inconvenience for them. I'd move them on and find others to work here if I knew I could find them."

- "If it cannot be done instantly then they don't bother. I hear things like 'isn't there an app for this?' or that it's going to take too long with the implication it is not worth starting. They are not interested in research beyond the first page of Google hits."

- "Their work ethic is in the wrong place. If I hear one more comment about 'work-life balance' I am going to scream. I agree that they need a better balance, and it should have more work in it than is currently the case."

- "They do not want to persevere at anything. If it gets too hard, they start looking at the online job boards. What is more, they do it in office hours on the equipment we have bought for them! That is not seen as a problem either."

- "Living at home forever is not good for them. They end up not knowing how the world works. Their disposable income is higher than a lot of those 10 to 20 years older, some of whom are their managers. It is hard to listen to them complain about the cost of living when they spend what they do in the local cafes. The humility and self-awareness are not there."

Leaving on time, not working outside contracted hours and not going for promotion are taken to be signs of laziness. But could there be something else going on?

No more mis-spent youth

One Friday evening a few years ago, I retraced my steps as a student at Manchester University with my best friend from that period. We revisited old haunts, walked the same streets and were allowed to visit the bar at the hall of residence in Rusholme where we first met decades ago. We did not expect to get in but found ourselves welcomed and directed up to the bar. We appreciated it, but also found it a little odd. Why would they want former students at least twice the age[1] of anyone else present to be taking up valuable bar space on a Friday night?

When we got to the bar, reality dawned. *They needed the trade.* A bunch of students walked out of the dining hall and, without even glancing across at the bar, went down the stairs. We had our quiet pint and left. Alcohol was not of interest to the young residents even on a Friday night. The same applied in the main student union up the road.

The neighbouring area was similarly quiet. Wilmslow Road's 'curry mile' felt incredible in the early '90s. The owner of my favourite curry house[2] once told me Rusholme had 273 restaurants between the university and the large hall of residence in Fallowfield. They were not all curry houses, but my recollection is that a high proportion of them were.

Their customer base was the local students and young professionals. At that point, Manchester was said to have 50,000 students, the largest concentration in Western Europe, the vast majority of whom were living away from home. There was Manchester University itself, Manchester Metropolitan University, UMIST, the Royal College of Music and the Royal College of Nursing. The early '90s was a brilliant time to live in the city, and many chose to stay after graduation. They kept the place busy every night from the early evening until the small hours as the students piled out of the clubs in town and found themselves hungry on the way home. I am not joking when I say that I had lived in the area for the best part of 10 years, and made umpteen visits, before I ate a curry before midnight.

---

1   Closer to three for some of them, but anyway.
2   This is Muky who originally worked in Shahenshah and then moved on to open up Shere Khan and others too. He arrived in Manchester from Pakistan around the same time I did from South Yorkshire with an incredible memory for people and an astute business brain.

The scene my friend and I found on this visit was markedly different. A number of curry houses survived, but they were the small minority, and many of them looked way beyond the reach of a student budget. When we walked back up the same street at pub closing time, the shutters were coming down. The pubs were quiet too. The Whitworth, known as a meeting place between the Moors Murderers[3], was closed and had converted into a coffee bar. It was the victim both of changing tastes and also Manchester City FC's move away from Maine Road to the stadium built for the Commonwealth Games.

I do not wish to portray myself as a hedonistic individual, but I more than enjoyed my late teens and early twenties. I started my university years hanging out with a similar rugby crowd to the one I had known from school, but within a year I had sought something different, spending my time in various music venues and finding my own space.

Gen X is no more a homogenous group than Gen Z, but I feel a little more comfortable stereotyping my own generation. I also acknowledge that only a fifth of school leavers made their way to university in those days, compared to just over half around the time[i] the oldest Gen Zs were graduating. In the early 1990s, it was seen as more of an achievement to get there rather than the standard.

That being the case, there is a limit on the extent to which I can claim my own experiences were typical for Gen X. I do remember some resentment among other Gen Xers who I knew and worked with in my summer jobs that they were working full-time and paying taxes for the university education of others who enjoyed a very different lifestyle.

---

3   One wonders how we ever saw this as a selling point, although it's not as if there was a blue plaque on the door. Ultimately, it was the pub over the road of the hall of residence, so when you were tired of looking at one bar, you moved to another. And evenings were spent in bars.

Nevertheless, I am going to describe my own experiences to make a point about the generation difference.

Gen X at university

Many of my fellow students saw lectures as entirely optional, particularly if any of them were foolishly arranged before 11:00 am or at any time on Fridays. Attendance at tutorials was much higher as your absence was more likely to be noticed in a smaller group. In a large lecture hall with hundreds of students, no one would pick this up, nor tried to do so.

Actual engagement with lectures would also be inconsistent. Late arrivals were common, often accompanied by excessive yawning, which indicated a busy evening the night before or a hangover. If anyone had the temerity to bring a laptop and tap away, they would be met with scorn as someone letting the side down. They were a rare sight at that time, and usually the property of mature students who would all sit together at the front and drown out the lectures en masse.

Academics made their own rules. One made it clear that he had no time for freeloaders. Students either paid attention in their lectures or were thrown out. He would set homework for his tutorials and those who arrived without theirs would be asked to leave. In this day and age that would be wholly reasonable and represent common sense, but back then it was a startling revelation. His colleagues treated him as an outlier, and the university let their staff apply whatever rules and practices they preferred.

Revision was an optional activity for many, particularly before your final year. An often scarce set of notes within an underused ring binder would be flicked through a few days in advance, at most. If you wanted to make an effort, a Pro Plus[4]-sponsored all-nighter was in order. I remember at the end of my first year getting up at 5:00 am to get some extra revision in for a 9:00 am examination to find my friend from the room next door arriving home from his night out. He also had a 9:00 am exam.[5]

Many students would also keep odd hours, usually not starting any work of any kind until after favourite daytime TV shows were over.[6] This was a luxury of the relative low cost of attending university. There were no tuition fees. Student loans only arrived in the early '90s and even then they were comparatively tiny. When the Student Loan Company was founded in 1990, the average loan per year was £390.[ii] In 2024, the estimated average total for a student over the course of their studies was £42,800[iii], of which approximately two-thirds would be for tuition fees of over £9,000 per year. Back in the day, I knew plenty who racked up debt, but it was generally not to pay for textbooks, rent or utilities.

Undertaking paid work to supplement income was comparatively rare, among my peers at least. Anyone who was compelled to join the actual working world attracted deep sympathy, particularly if the number of hours per week drifted into double figures. Not only was this seen as an unfathomable hardship, but it also generated

---

4   Pro Plus kept you alert, allegedly. Coffee was much less of a pursuit in those days. It was years before the first chain coffee shops hit the UK. I remember visiting Seattle in the late '90s and staring at commuters carrying a cup on the way to the office. *'This is the future'*, I thought.

5   He passed; I did not. So, where's the moral in that story? Anyway, that's you, Vijay.

6   Why we spent so many hours watching *Going for Gold* or *Neighbours* is anyone's guess. But they were easy watching and provided topics to talk about in the evening.

the incredible inconvenience of having to get changed and make yourself presentable. Lounging about in whatever clothes you slept in the night before until the bar opened in the early evening was pretty standard.

Thousands of students experienced what was, in effect, a state-sponsored party for much of their university lives. This also says something about who was going to university. Rent, food and bills still had to be paid for, but the vast majority of people I knew, including me, had all that sorted out for them by their parents. The cost of going to university is not a completely new issue.

It was a carefree existence, and we were all allowed to get on with our formative years without it being preserved for posterity on social media. There are fewer than 20 photographs of me in my university days, and over half of those were taken in one evening. None of them show me in a positive light, particularly those from the small hours.

Even before university days, it was not seen as a significant issue if you did not do much work for your GCSEs[7] or A levels, particularly for the better off in society. You could retake your examinations as one option, go to a crammer[8], start work and do them again or just not bother. A high proportion of the people you might work for had

---

7   Here is a Gen X dividing line. Based on the years I have used for Gen X, half of us did GCSEs, which started in 1988. Anyone in the older half did O levels. For years, the latter half were told that our examinations were too easy and our grades were not comparable with theirs. This was particularly irritating for me as around half of my cohort at university had taken a year out, whereas I went straight to university from school, so I heard this all the time from those sitting in the same lecture halls.

8   Definitely for the privileged few, this one. They could cost big bucks, for the time at least, and have faded from the scene.

no university education, so a degree was not seen as essential. A narrative of 'not taking university seriously because work was the real business' might even do you a favour.

In the early '90s, there was no sense of 'globalisation' by our modern definition, including the idea that those from other countries might take your jobs without having to move to the UK. The economic rise of Japan was seen as a real threat, and anyone who went as far as trying to learn the language was viewed as a no-nonsense visionary who had no limit on their ambition or lifetime earnings.

Life-changing technological advances were not particularly on the horizon, despite what we thought at the time when we rented our 'picture in picture' TV from Rumbelows. Mobile phones were not commonplace, and even those who had one could only use it for telephone calls, text messages and the occasional game of Snake.[9]

The recession of the early '90s was definitely viewed as a problem, and its presence was a key factor in my choice of teaching as a career, but it was considered as a temporary problem. My generation's progression from university examinations to well-paid professions was not considered at risk as long as you eventually got your head down and did some work.

Not everyone at university was the same. There was an extremely significant disparity in expectations between different courses. Anyone insane enough to sign up for an engineering degree was working two to three times as many hours as the average person

---

9   A low-resolution video game where you manoeuvred an ever-growing line around a blank screen and avoided crashing into yourself. By modern standards, inexplicably basic. Back then the prospect of a new high score was an unmatched white knuckle ride. Such were the times.

on my social science course. Battling through to the first year's examinations was a serious test of mettle as well as brainpower and ingenuity. That did not mean they stayed away from the bar or the nightclub; they just survived on less sleep and more alcohol in their system for their morning lectures than was conducive to engaging with that level of mathematics.

Gen X's experience of early professional life

When it came to early years as young professionals, standards were also very different to today. Arriving at work a little hungover from the night before was not viewed as a faux pas, as long as you did not do it too often. Not doing so on Friday was considered a missed opportunity given you only had one day to get through. I tended not to do that too often, but a pub lunch with a beer on a Friday was the custom, and then back to school to teach in the afternoon. That was with a group who were around twice my age, who took me under their wing and showed me how it was done.

For those who smoked, how many fag breaks you might be permitted was a key part of your informal terms and conditions. It was a lifestyle choice in the same way as if you wore brown or black shoes, and workplaces were expected to accommodate it as a basic human right.

Given all this, I find it extremely hard to listen to my peers talking about students and young professionals not working hard enough. So many of them enjoyed years of an incredibly cheap and carefree university experience and did not have to work anything like as hard for it. Beyond that, early professional life was often no different to that of a student.

They also enjoyed the reassurance that if they put some money aside from the salary of their first 'proper job', in a few short years, they could have their own place and avoid paying what was called the 'dead money' of rent. They were also able to start professional life debt-free or close to it, and therefore in a position to save rather than paying off the interest.

When I graduated, less than half of all students achieved an upper second degree or better. First-class degrees in particular were extremely rare and the sanctuary of either the unnaturally gifted or those who had by-passed all the fun. You really stood out if you had one of those. I remember that it also aroused some suspicion amongst others about the priorities in your life if university had been solely about work. I still have the list from my university and there were 4 first class degrees out of approximately 300 on the course.

Changes in behaviour over time

As time went on, this started to change. I used to say about the generation we now call Millennials that they were the first generation to be better behaved than the one before, and it shifted further over the years.

In my Gen X youth, I got used to seeing grainy footage of the post-war moral panics such as the Teddy Boys, followed by the swinging '60s, and Timothy Leary advising all others to 'turn on, tune in and drop out'. Then there was punk, the battles between mods and rockers as represented in the film *Quadrophenia*, and the trend of vandalising VW cars so people could wear the badge round their neck in the same way as the Beastie Boys.

This is just a small selection. A general lack of respect for parents and other elders was one theme, as was a perceived lack of appreciation for wartime sacrifices. Popular headlines have always come from ideas such as 'kids have it too easy these days', 'young people today are badly behaved' or 'teenagers are worse than they used to be'. That was just as true for Gen X growing up in the '80s as it is now.

This was followed by peak holiday antics in early adult life. The rented bedroom was traded for the beach as a place to sleep during the day, with nightlife to follow. Hotel rooms were for suitcase storage.[10] It is hard to comprehend now what members of my generation subjected themselves to and imposed on others, but suffice to say it wasn't healthy.

When cameras were added to phones and social media emerged, the saying 'what goes on tour stays on tour' no longer applied. Thomas Cook stopped their Club 18-30 packages in 2018 as it was no longer in keeping with the brand. All of this behaviour happened in person, rather than through a screen, with no prospect of it being recorded. The dangers and implications of the online world will be covered in Chapter 4.

I was part of the last cohort of young people to go through university without the internet. I then spent the first decade of my career barely using email. You might wonder why it took so long. The reason was that the speeds of dial-up and computer processors were a major barrier to doing anything at the time. The network manager at my second school used to type out notes, make copies and put them in pigeon holes. One local authority ran a project in a few schools that meant everyone in the council had to avoid using their computer on Tuesday afternoons.

As inefficient as all this seems, we were also protected in a way we could not appreciate at the time. It is true that technology enabled many tasks to be carried out much more quickly, most obviously when communicating with individual colleagues who often had to be found in person to get a message across. It also created new tasks and much higher expectations about productivity, often accompanied

---

10   I'm not claiming first-hand experience here, and truth be told it was
      never for me.

by numbers in the form of real-time data, metrics, key performance indicators and dashboards. Gen X blissfully missed out on this in young professional life. Can we really call Gen Z lazy, or is there now a much higher and more complex bar?

Impact of globalisation

As tuition costs began to be met by individuals rather than governments and student debt spiralled, the idea of paying off university costs over an entire working life made little sense unless it was going to be taken seriously. This was particularly when globalisation arrived and led to more competition from abroad, outsourcing and a greater sense of dispensability.

The price of rent used to be a small step up from student accommodation, and often not even that. This changed dramatically. Saving for a property deposit started its shift from the responsible thing to do to an impossible dream.

Changes also came to schools. 'League tables' raised expectations among governing bodies and parents. Ofsted was in its infancy in the mid-1990s. The concept that visitors from an independent regulator could be permitted to visit your classroom and make recommendations for how your practice could improve was novel. It was also met with very strong resistance from plenty, some of whom may not have had a lesson observation for decades. In the staffroom at break on my first day, I was told by everyone that the last person who sat in my seat had been 'forced out' following the recent inspection. Expectations shifted, and levels of accountability rose with them.

The required grades to get into university courses started to move upwards. Failing at school and then sorting yourself out further down the line remained possible for those who found their niche later in life but was also far less wise. Parental pressure increased as the life chances of their children became more precarious.

Gen Z behaviour at school and beyond

As a result of these higher expectations, compared to Generation X, the young people I worked with were far more dedicated, tenacious and better behaved. They have stayed that way as they entered higher education and the workplace.

One example is the percentage of people in the UK who have smoked over time. Partly, this is the outcome of price, advertising bans and health education, but that is not the whole picture. The percentage of smokers across the whole population dropped from 45% in the mid-1970s to 15% in the mid-2010s.[iv]

	2011	2020
18 to 24	26%	12%
25 to 34	26%	15%
35 to 44	23%	15%
45 to 54	22%	14%
55 to 64	19%	13%
65+	10%	7%

Figure 5: Proportion who were current smokers by age group, UK, 2011 to 2020[11]

---

11   This does not include vapes. It is a moot point, but although vapes are definitely not risk-free, the evidence so far is that they are far less harmful.

Over the 2010s, the percentage of smokers in each age group fell, but it was the youngest year group where it dropped most sharply; 18-24-year-olds went from being the joint largest group of smokers to the second lowest. Those who are 65 years or older have the fewest smokers for two reasons: either they have finally given up as they approached the autumn of their years or they did not survive to do so.

Alcohol follows a similar trend. In 2021, NHS England reported that more than half (55%) of all adults reported had consumed alcohol in the last week, but only 37% of 16 to 24 year olds had done so compared to over 60% of those aged between 55 and 75[v].

Figures from the Institute of Alcohol Studies showed that the number of units consumed by 16 to 24 year olds had halved from 2000 to 2016 yet it had risen for every age group from 35 upwards.[vi] Market intelligence agency Mintel reports that 'around a third of people aged 18-24 do not drink alcohol at all, but those who do tend to drink primarily as a treat, to relax, or to mark a special occasion'.[vii] The same article describes Gen Z as a 'sober, curious generation'.

The front-facing camera became more widely available in 2003. As uptake increased over the next decade, particularly when one was added to the iPhone 4 in 2010, the rise of the selfie meant that how you looked mattered more and more. With apps like Instagram, WhatsApp, Snapchat and TikTok[12] taking off, Gen Z behaviour was going to be on show far more often. Looking hungover with nicotine-stained teeth was not an image to portray, particularly when people realised that a snapshot had an infinite viewing lifespan.

---

12   The timeline is often lost here, but TikTok only came out in 2017. WhatsApp, Instagram and Snapchat were launched in consecutive years from 2009 to 2011.

Evidence shows that Gen Z is also much less likely to participate in casual sex and fighting. It is hard to believe that this is not as a result of a drop in alcohol consumption. Oasis' song 'Cigarettes and Alcohol' starts with a line about their discovery representing Noel Gallagher finally finding 'something worth living for'. That struck a chord far more with Gen X in the mid-1990s than would be the case now.

Social media, and the ubiquitous presence of the camera, is a key reason as to why Gen Z behaviour has improved. The whole concept of 24/7 reputation management grew with this generation of digital natives. Unlike Millennials, they have been managing perceptions of themselves online from a very young age. Enforcement of the minimum age for signing up to social media accounts by the platforms has been weak, and that is putting it politely. Not only that, but Gen Z's parents increasingly used the same technology, enabling them to show off how well their children were doing. Societal pressure around parenting grew along with the pressure of this on Gen Z behaviour. This has implications for the workplace, as I will discuss in later chapters.

Gen X was able to behave without any fear of a legacy. There would be no fear that your activities would be captured in the pub, nightclub or on a dance floor and shared with an employer at the time or decades down the line. You can never be certain now that you are out of the public gaze, or whether you are being recorded.

Everyone having their own camera permanently in their pocket is only part of the story. The ability to capture a fuller picture via video and audio has also significantly affected behaviour. An image may go viral but video is far more powerful and potentially damaging. The camera does not have to be pointing directly at you to capture a set of moments you would rather were not captured at all.

The first iPhone was released in 2007 when the oldest Gen Zs were 10 years old. Social media may have preceded the smartphone, but its proliferation accelerated sharply as accounts could be accessed and updated on the move. The unfortunate truth is that Gen Z had technology and software their parents and teachers were not equipped to support. The power of it all was not understood, and the risks we are acutely aware of today were not anticipated.

When the front-facing camera arrived in the mass market, Facebook had 500 million global accounts. Of these, a mere 30% of users were accessing it on their phones.[viii] The trend for selfies took off and has never dimmed. The pressure to stay presentable so you could take a selfie at any time influenced behaviour, as did the idea that somewhere a camera was watching you in shops and high streets.

Before smartphones facilitated the global explosion in social media use, 'viruses' were seen as a much bigger issue than 'viral' content. The world had not learned how to use it, and the companies themselves had little sense of the regulation it might require. The *IT Crowd* episode 'Friendface' in 2008 wincingly showed how adults across the land started out on social media by checking out their school friends of the past.

It is interesting to look back at the timeline of some of the major social media players and how the market has developed in response to consumer needs. The value of Snapchat's disappearing posts is obvious for those who do not want a lifetime imprint for every employer to see. The same is true of applications where users choose who sees their posts, and has a record of who has done so. It is hard to believe that TikTok is so young, but it clearly filled a gap with Gen Z in mind.

Generation Z has had a lot to manage with greater online threats and a far less secure future. This has had a positive impact on their behaviour in teenage and adult life, but it does mean they are more reluctant to try something new, mindful of where and how they use their energy and more worried about failing publicly. While Gen X can perceive these behaviours as lazy, because of their own upbringing and context, Gen Z can be cautious, smart and image-conscious. Plus, for those Gen Zers who choose to work for an organisation, they need support from the older generation if they're going to succeed. Let's turn to a key strategy now.

Make professional development more personal

"We have weekly one-to-ones and we also have quarterly reviews. We like to sit down with a manager and look back on performance, but also discuss where we want to be in the next quarter. It's really helpful to have those feedback structures. We also get some transparency in terms of where we are all going and can contribute to it. It is really key because it helps us to develop."

Gen Zer

Organisations that wish to support their performance-conscious young employees need to be prepared to engage with their development on a personal and professional level. **I strongly recommend organisations offer a very broad range of development opportunities.**

Gen Z's hunger for learning and improvement is well represented in their outstanding academic outcomes. Companies that ensure their new employees can continue on this trajectory, and that also make clear what is on offer from the very start, will be in a good position.

There are two key aspects to 'personal' development. The first is personal in the sense of personalised, or bespoke. Although younger employees will have common needs, they will also expect some choice and to be treated as individuals. These may reflect particular interests, or areas that may serve their future career.

It is hard to overestimate the extent to which online activity has enabled life to become more personalised over the course of a generation. There are zillions of internet rabbit holes to dive down, social media accounts to follow and engage with, and a streaming music collection to curate.

The secondary school experience in England has not followed this personalised experience.[13] The arrival of the English Baccalaureate[14] in 2010, and its use as a performance measure, restricted the choices for many Gen Z students across England. The diversity of choice in higher education remains strong in terms of both location and content. There are over 100 universities offering a history degree in the UK, with an average of 13 courses each.[ix]

The growth of online learning and thought leadership via social media provides younger employees with a huge choice beyond

---

13   The National Curriculum had last been revised in 2014. The Labour government elected in 2024 are taking a look.

14   Briefly, the EBACC, as it came to be known, meant a student should take English (language), English literature, mathematics, history or geography, two sciences and a language. The Department for Education (DfE) set a target for 75% of pupils to enter the EBACC by 2022 and 90% by 2025. For schools who insisted on the EBACC as the default, their students had one or two subjects to choose from elsewhere. A number of subjects were squeezed out. I remember a governing body meeting where we went round the table and no one had the EBACC, including me. It was a high-powered group too, including senior civil servants and a former head of marketing at IBM. For the record, I did two languages, both history and geography and one science.

the workplace. Vast quantities are available for free in the form of podcasts, blogs and e-books. Much of it acts as a loss leader for materials and training that come at a cost, and it would be an abdication of duty to leave it all to the employee.

In this respect, organisations can take two key actions.

First, provide a forum for employees to bring to the table what they have read and learned from elsewhere. It is up to the organisation whether this is a compulsory activity, not least because it carries an implication of employees engaging in work beyond their contracted hours. There is the option to make it compulsory to attend, but not prepare for, as long there are enough ideas to bring to the table.

Second, have at least one senior person in the room to see what is coming through. This is so leaders can find out what their employees are listening to and to learn something themselves. Organisations need to find out the best of what is available and consult with staff on what they want. The paid versions of the free content can be expensive, but still represent good value. Managers and employees can collectively determine what is most useful for the next step of anyone's professional development and allocate working hours for employees to pursue it.

Leaders can also do themselves a favour by engaging with this material themselves. A senior manager who read a few 'management classics' in their formative years but nothing since, and who does not engage in new ideas via social media either, might be treated by Gen Z staff with some suspicion. You do not have to try going viral with an amusing or unusual TikTok video, although I imagine it would be fun for your young employees to watch.[15]

---

15   Fun at best actually. 'Cringe' is most likely the reaction you will get.

On top of that is the kind of line management practice described in the quote at the start of this section, where employees are made to feel they have genuine ownership over their own development. A traditional line management process tends to focus primarily on performance. If development is part of the conversation, the focus will be on professional needs. Personal needs matter too, and any model where they are absent from the conversation has severe limits.

Gen Z's academic outcomes may be far beyond those of previous generations, but that also comes as a result of a school curriculum that focuses on qualifications to a great extent. Personal development may form part of the Ofsted inspection framework in England, but it does not contribute to examination scores. The gains in examination outcomes have not been matched by similar gains in personal development.

The fact that personal development, or, as it is often called, Personal Social and Health Education (PSHE), is not a compulsory subject[16] at all might surprise some. The Children and Social Work Act (2020) introduced compulsory relationships education in primary schools and compulsory relationships and sex education in secondary schools. Health education, both mental and physical, became statutory across primary and secondary schools.[x] The older half of Gen Z were, however, out of school by the time the 2020 Act was passed into law.

The law also leaves a long list of topics where schools should 'tailor their local PSHE programme to reflect the needs of their pupils'.[xi] While

---

16   This is in England. The education systems across England, Wales, Scotland and Northern Ireland vary more than is often considered the case. This is not a book about education, but if it was I would spend some time justifying an argument that England has fallen behind the others in the value of personal development education.

there is an argument that this flexibility is welcome, it also leaves open the possibility of a lack of meaningful coverage, which means school leavers are ill-equipped for aspects of adult life including the workplace.

The nature of social media algorithms also presents a considerable challenge in that it is difficult for teachers and parents to see what children are viewing. The responsive nature of social media platforms means that what you see next depends on what you have already seen.

Getting inside the experience of today's teenagers cannot be done unless you have their phone in your hand. It is only when you see what they are being shown that you can start to deduce what they have already clicked on or watched for an extended period.[17] Even then it is hard to separate the impact of their previous activity from what they are being shown because of their age and what is popular with their peers.

Fending for themselves

The pressure for schools to achieve excellent academic outcomes has also been a factor in the disastrous deterioration in the mental health of teenagers. An NHS report in 2022 showed that 26% of 17-19-year-olds in England have a 'probable mental health disorder'. Five years previously, it was 10%. Covid did not help, but the 250%+ rise in five years is not just down to this. In 2023, NHS statistics showed that the same also applied to 20% of 8-16-year-olds.

---

17   I will mention it in the footnotes so I don't have to bring any more attention to him than necessary, but Andrew Tate is the classic example of this. I visited a bunch of schools across England and Scotland in summer 2023 for another project, and he was named as the biggest issue they were facing in all of them. Students, particularly the boys, knew who he was, but the adults were oblivious until the issues started to manifest.

Collectively, Gen Z arrived at their young professional years less prepared for the workplace than those who come before them. This pressure for schools to maximise their examination results also led to a reduction in work experience placements, with schools reluctant to give away valuable curriculum time to activities without qualifications attached.

The tendency for schools to offer intervention sessions after school hours, on Saturday and during school holidays also left less room for the employment experience gained by working in shops and doing paper rounds. It is true that those who go to university are engaging in paid work more than was the case decades ago, but undergraduates working in shops, pubs and coffee shops are not gaining experience in workplaces they may hope to join after university. Work experience placements at school may not have generated income, but those who spent time in the kinds of organisations they wanted to work in down the line gained valuable experience.

Work, but not in a workplace

Beyond the lack of work experience, the internet has enabled many ways of earning money that do not involve physically attending a workplace. The trend for buying and selling vintage clothes online has been profitable for many, but it does not involve having to work with others two or three times your age, negotiating the protocols of staffroom fridges or line management meetings.

Employers may find that expectations around working etiquette such as dress code and email conventions need to be made more explicit than they might think reasonable. As Gen Xers, we developed our soft skills together as adults as the technology arrived after the beginning of our working lives. Gen Z did not. They now learn it *after* they have been engaged in social media with their peers for years. There is a big difference. If in doubt, spell it out.

Gen X managers should also be prepared to discuss their expectations with their younger colleagues, not demand that life must remain as it was for them when they started. A stubborn reluctance to move with the times will likely create as much eye-rolling from Gen Z as anything else. Gen X managers may have a more of a battle in staying relevant than they imagine.

Managers may have more than a few 'do I really have to?' moments as they find themselves having to go through aspects of work they did not have to previously explain. You should spare them (and you too, for that matter) the 'you have a first-class degree but you don't know how to do X?' type conversations. Particularly so if you do not wish to have the roles reversed with various 'you've been working here for 15 years and you do not know who/what this is?' questions in return.

Ultimately, if you want your Gen Z staff to know something, do not assume it will be learned by osmosis or that it will have been picked up through a pre-working-life era that was very different to yours. Even at the time of writing, work experience is 'expected' at school, but not 'statutory', although 'encounters with employers and employees' and 'experiences of workplaces' are now statutory.

The Gatsby Benchmarks, which 'define what world class careers provision in education looks like'[18], were a fine initiative but were only made statutory in 2018, again some time after the oldest Gen Z had moved on from school. The fact that they were introduced during a decade when school budgets were falling did not help. Schools

---

18   The Gatsby Benchmarks form a framework for organising careers
      provision at schools and colleges.

might have been able to tick the boxes, but not necessarily offer a quality experience.

The focus on academic qualifications rather than personal development has led to an imbalance and a greater development deficit than was the case for previous generations. Your Gen Z employees may come to you with a far higher level of technical skills, the ability to engage in electronic multitasking beyond your comprehension and, let us not forget, qualifications, but there may be other aspects that aren't there.

If you want your young employees to have the 'real world' skills necessary for success in your industry, then you need to be prepared to provide them through training, and not make assumptions that they will arrive with those skills built in.

Consider doing this training within a more intensive and longer induction programme than you might be used to providing. On the other side, you should be prepared for your Gen Zs to want to get this right more than you might envisage. They know they need high-level interpersonal skills for their futures and may have a strong sense that their education and other life experiences to date have not provided them. Employers and employees have common interests here.

As an employer, you do not need to tiptoe around this. Indeed, if you did, it would most likely raise questions about your transparency. When a very high proportion of a person's communication has been asynchronous, which by definition means 'not in person', they have had less practice in live conversations about work or thinking on their feet. Gen Z has had a lot more experience in multitasking, but when it comes to a single, uninterrupted activity, not so much. This includes digital skills. Gen Z may be digital natives, but that does not mean they have the precise digital literacy skills you need them to have from the beginning.

The fact that they have grown up with a variety of screens and a multitude of tools does not mean they know how to use them all or how they might be applied to resolve a particular problem. Not every issue can be solved digitally.

Tech, critical thinking and multitasking

An overreliance on tools can also mitigate the kind of critical thinking employers need from employees. The emergence and explosion of everyday artificial intelligence tools only amplifies this issue. An understanding of how to get a tool to operate and deliver the outcome you want is not the same as solving a problem. Sometimes a tool has to be created or adapted rather than just plucked from an electronic shelf.

Critical thinking skills are highly prized by employers and they form the basis of your decision-making when hiring. By critical thinking I mean information literacy skills such as research and source evaluation, and others such as problem-solving, conflict resolution, communication, analysis and so on.

Do not underestimate Gen Z's hunger to work on their areas for development. They may make progress not only faster than you imagined, but also quicker than others with more experience and expertise within the organisation. Just because they may not have the basics in one key aspect does not mean they cannot rapidly reach an advanced level with the right resources in place. The work ethic that led to the explosion in first-class degrees is at your disposal.

Growing up in an age when computing power has developed so quickly has meant that Gen Z is able to process information at lightning speed, compared to earlier generations. They also have far more experience at having to separate fact from fiction. Everyone has to be so much sharper in that respect these days, but it is only the youngest generation in the workplace who arrive at work with a decade-plus experience.

Gen Z is not immune to the idea that a lot of time spent on social media may not have prepared them for an employer's demands. They will want to know the scenarios they are going to come across, and how they might tackle them. Where that involves critical thinking skills, judgement and intuition, tell them so. Give them an opportunity to practise. If the answer involved an algorithmic approach, they wouldn't have expected you to hire a human to do it anyway.

This argument can run two ways. The idea of Gen Z as a 'hypercognitive generation' has also brought criticism. The teenage bedroom with a laptop, potentially more than one screen both with 10 to 20 windows open on each, plus a phone screen ever filling with notifications, can be interpreted in two ways.

One is that having so much open at any given time comes as a result of a lack of both memory and concentration span. *Time* magazine[xii] once ran a headline that 'you have the memory of a goldfish', approximately nine seconds.

On the other hand, I would argue that Gen Z is a 'hypercognitive generation' with the agility to filter and process at speed. It is multitasking at a whole new level. Yet this is often portrayed as a concentration problem, as in the case of the famous *Time* headline.

Yet if Gen Z really could not concentrate, they would not be producing so many first-class degrees from a series of three-hour written examinations. Stories about a lack of memory or concentration span makes for good copy, but it does not stack up with my experience. I remember being told about a child who apparently 'couldn't concentrate for two seconds' in any classroom, but would also arrive very tired on Monday morning having put in 18-hour shifts on the new *Call of Duty* over the weekend. We have seen the same with Netflix and a 'just one more episode' mentality for a favourite show. Soon it's the season finale, which turns out to be two and a half hours, resulting in a 3:00 am bedtime.

The ability to flick endlessly between different windows or through a TikTok feed may not necessarily be productive, but it is unlikely to be a barrier for your Gen Zs becoming the young professionals you need. There may be advantages to your professional development programmes being broken down segment by segment, but do not feel everything has to be in tiny packages because that is all they can cope with. Short videos, highly structured programmes and concise documentation can be helpful so it can be easily digested, and returned to, but is it not necessary to provide professional development two minutes at a time. I have seen it made into a big issue, but for me it is a non-issue. Don't let it constrain you.

The organisations that are prepared to rethink the breadth and depth of what is on offer, and liaise with their employees as they do so, can expect to be rewarded for their efforts. If you make the effort to look past the Myth of Lazy, you will find a generation ready and willing to engage.

Endnotes

i   Coughlan, S. (2019, September 26). *The symbolic target of 50% at university reached.* BBC News. https://www.bbc.co.uk/news/education-49841620

ii   *Student finance through the ages.* (n.d.). https://spotlight.leeds.ac.uk/thanks-to-you-2024/could-you-live-on-50p-a-week/student-finance-through-the-ages/index.html#:~:text=In%201990%20the%20Student%20Loans,loan%20value%20was%20%C2%A3390

iii   *Student loan forecasts for England, Financial year 2023-24.* (2024, June 27). Explore Education Statistics – GOV.UK. https://explore-education-statistics.service.gov.uk/find-statistics/student-loan-forecasts-for-england

iv   Brookman, R. N. a. A. (2021, December 7). *Smoking prevalence in the UK and the impact of data collection changes – Office for National Statistics.*https://www.ons.gov.uk/peoplepopulationandcommunity/healthandsocialcare/drugusealcoholandsmoking/bulletins/smokingprevalenceintheukandtheimpactofdatacollectionchanges/2020#:~:text=In%20Quarter%201%20and%20Quarters,with%20any%20other%20age%20group.

v   NHS England (2022, Dec 21) *Health Survey for England, 2021 part 1.* https://digital.nhs.uk/data-and-information/publications/statistical/health-survey-for-england/2021

vi   Angus, C. (2019, January 25). *A generation of hidden drinkers: What's happening to the drinking of the over 50s?* Institute of Alcohol Studies. https://www.ias.org.uk/2019/01/25/a-generation-of-hidden-drinkers-whats-happening-to-the-drinking-of-the-over-50s/

vii   *Gen Z: The Sober Curious Generation | Mintel.* (2024, January 17). Mintel. https://www.mintel.com/insights/food-and-drink/gen-z-sober-curious-generation/

viii   Wikipedia contributors. (2025, March 14). *Facebook.* Wikipedia. https://en.wikipedia.org/wiki/Facebook#:~:text=In%202010%2C%20Facebook%20won%20the,the%20site%20from%20mobile%20devices

ix   Sana. (n.d.). *Compare the best university degrees courses UK | WhatUni.* https://www.whatuni.com/

x   *What is PSHE education?* (n.d.). https://pshe-association.org.uk/what-is-pshe-education

xi   *Personal, social, health and economic (PSHE) education.* (2021, September 13). GOV.UK. https://www.gov.uk/government/publications/personal-social-health-and-economic-education-pshe/personal-social-health-and-economic-pshe-education

xii   McSpadden, K. (2015, May 14). You now have a shorter attention span than a goldfish. *TIME.* https://time.com/3858309/attention-spans-goldfish/2015

4

The Myth of Unreliable

"Some of the interviews with those in their twenties are a complete waste of time. They seem to have no idea how they should prepare, or if they should prepare at all. They do not look the part either. Some of them walk in and I feel like sending them straight back out."

Gen X employer

This chapter covers the heart of the idea of the Snowflake concept, the idea of Gen Z being flaky, clueless, even entitled. None of those options quite captured what I wanted to convey, though, and here's why.

'Clueless' infers that Gen Z arrives in the workplace knowing less about the working world than any previous generation. 'Flaky' suggests they have a tenuous relationship with what is required in the workplace. Finally, 'entitled' betrays that Gen Z has unrealistic expectations about what they can achieve in the working world. This entitlement is expressed further in how 'the world revolves around them', that it is up to older generations to teach, and that Gen Z don't prepare themselves independently. Variations on this include that 'young people today see themselves as special' and therefore inherently deserving of special treatment.

All of this boils down to the name I have given this myth, the Myth of Unreliable, because the accusation that 'Gen Z cannot be relied upon' is the most prevalent of all. And, in my mind, the most insulting.

Workplace observations

These are examples of what I hear from my peers and in the media.

- "Some of our staff have their own business outside of work. It causes real issues with their commitment to the job. Moonlighting used to be frowned upon. They just don't understand why."
- "They want to change plans at the last minute, but do not expect it to be challenged. They do not understand the value of reliability, or the impact it causes others when they pull out or disappear."
- "They expect their mental health to be prized at all costs by everyone around them. Pressure with deadlines leads to requests for mental health days as though it was an entitlement."
- "Interviews are a real problem. They apply for a job, are offered an interview and then do not show up. Some who have been appointed do not turn up to start work on day one so the whole process starts again. They just ghost us. Who do they think they are?"
- "They have a real issue with having their cameras on for meetings. They consider it to be totally unreasonable. Then when we say we want to limit working from home so we can see them, that's an even bigger problem."
- "If it cannot be done on their phone, and quickly, they seem to think it cannot be done at all. The attitude seems to be that if the task was important there would be an app for it."
- "When I tell them there is an issue with something they have done, they cannot believe it. They turn it on me saying that they should

have been supported better and given more training. Sorry, but some things you have to work out yourself. I cannot hold their hand through everything. I do not want to either. Learning from mistakes is really important at work."

- "They live on their phones, always talking to their friends, but they have no experience of talking to anyone else. When an older person wants to talk to them, they cannot handle it. They just look at the floor."
- "They are very reluctant, often to the point of a blank refusal, to undertake any task for which they have not been trained."
- "We had one who could not understand why we had an expectation of not talking about aspects of our work online. They expect to be able to broadcast everything 24/7 and for us to be happy with it. They could not believe they were held to account and investigated."

A pragmatic generation

Given the significance of this myth to my overall argument, I am going to refer to two key characteristics of Gen Z rather than one.

First, I am going to discuss Gen Z's tendency to be pragmatic. This one comes first because it pushes back hardest on the Myth of Unreliable. It also generates more of the after-chat from my speaking engagements than any other. This may be because it covers the aspects where Gen X and others discover they are furthest away from seeing the world through Gen Z's eyes.

The idea that Gen Z is pragmatic often does not sit well with older generations. When I talk, I can see grimaces and raised eyebrows all around the room. It jars with what can be hardened perceptions around Gen Z's idealism, entrepreneurial spirit and the entitlement I referenced at the beginning of this chapter. The initial response is often bewilderment around why bailing on a job interview could ever be a measured response. For clarity, I am not arguing for this case and will respond to some of those points more directly in the section about apprehension.

I argue that Gen Z's pragmatism is not just a key characteristic, but also a foundation for other characteristics. It is a true standout. If you want to understand this generation, you need to understand this.

Secondly, I will address the points about mental health and everything else that comes under the propensity to be apprehensive. It is hard to overstate how important this issue is to Gen Z and why they need to see it matter to their managers and leaders.

Rise of the solopreneur

In recent years, there has been an explosion in the number of individuals setting up their own businesses and other enterprises. The term 'solopreneur' defines this group a little more precisely. A solopreneur is 'the sole owner and employee of a business, and is responsible for all aspects of its management and organisation'. If you are thinking that this sounds exactly like a sole trader, or a single-person limited company, I would say you have a point. I would also argue that this was always entrepreneurial activity.

A traditional view of an entrepreneur was someone who wanted to start out on their own, then grow a company into a large enterprise with a huge body of staff, offices around the globe and millions in profit. It is the story of Oprah Winfrey's ascent from presenting her local news programme to a global media empire or Richard Branson from his mail-order record business to a multinational conglomerate. Solopreneurs are different in that they stay small, and most frequently operate online, selling services or products. They will use other organisations' services but are rarely bricks-and-mortar businesses.

They want to grow, and often operate globally, but not through a physical presence around the world or through building a large body of staff. Sometimes they are aligned to major brands.

The figures below highlight the progress of solopreneurs on one well-known example. Etsy is an e-commerce platform, with a particular focus on handmade items and vintage goods, amongst others. It started in 2005. The number of Etsy buyers grew fivefold from just over 9 million worldwide in 2012 to 46 million in 2019. By 2021 it had doubled again to over 96 million.[i]

Undoubtedly, the Covid-19 pandemic was the key factor in the number of Etsy businesses increasing at this scale in the latter period. When faced with time on their hands, and uncertainty over future prospects, millions more took the plunge and sold their talents online. The number of Etsy businesses have since stabilised, rather than fallen backwards. This is because setups like Etsy are here to stay, as is this model of earning income.

Remember that the pandemic was not the first significant increase. The number of individual Etsy sellers had already increased very substantially in advance of the pandemic. Some of this can be attributed to growing awareness of the platform and the means of using it, but not all.

This graph includes all sellers, but the demographics are particularly revealing. The report shows that 86% of Etsy sellers were women. More relevant to this book, they were twice as likely to be under 35 than the owners of all other businesses. In addition, those on low incomes were also far more common; this most frequently correlates with the young. Gen Z is a big part of driving the Etsy boom.[ii]

Etsy is just one example. Another is Depop, which describes itself as a 'community-powered circular fashion marketplace'. While Etsy is about the handmade, Depop rewards those with an eye for a bargain that they can sell on for a profit, particularly vintage clothing. If any of the details in this book are making you feel old, bear this in mind: for an item to count as 'vintage', it must be at least 20 years old. This brings the beginning of this century into the vintage category. All of this for a platform with 26 million users where 90% of its users are Gen Z.

The table below from Companies House shows the number of new companies (or 'incorporations' – dark line) against the number of dissolutions (light line) since the late 1970s.

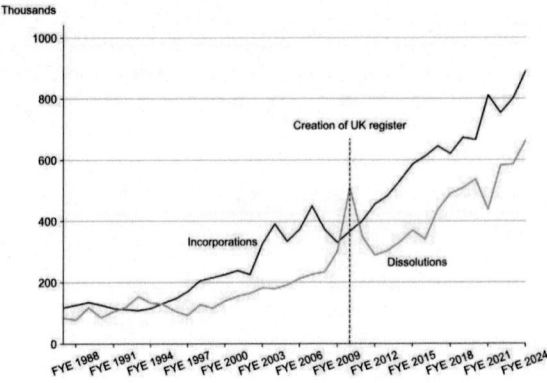

Figure 6: Number of new companies/dissolutions in the UK 1998 to 2024[iii]

Over time, technology has made it easier for new companies to be incorporated, but that does not wholly explain the steep incline within the graph. The number of new companies has not always outpaced the number of dissolutions, although those times are restricted to times of economic recession. The pandemic may have maintained and extended a trend, but it did not create it.

Companies House does not offer a demographic breakdown of directors and other 'persons with significant control'. Given that many of the new businesses in recent years generate income through Etsy, Depop or similar platforms, it is highly probable that the youngest generation are disproportionately represented here. As referenced in the introduction, somewhere between quarter and half a million Gen Zs are currently named as a director at Companies House.

The acceleration also coincided with Gen Z coming into the workplace. By April 2024, approximately half of companies were five years old or younger, and almost three-quarters less than ten years old[iv].

Santander published research[v] in 2024 that three quarters of Gen Z are seeking to be 'their own boss'. The equivalent figure in 2023 was 64% who said they wanted to run their own business.[vi] This in itself was a 50% increase from the 42% survey published by recruitment website Monster several years previously, which also reported on the extent to which Gen Zs were 'concerned about long-term prospects' and sought 'multiple streams of income out of necessity'.

Even the lowest figure of 42% was ten points higher than for any other generation surveyed at the time. As every cohort of Gen Z becomes old enough to hit the workplace, the more they want to run their own gig.

Part of the rationale for wanting your own business is that the barriers to entry of setting up on your own are very low. A group of friends can meet for coffee on Saturday morning and have an idea for a business. They decide to sell the product or service online, at least as a starting point. There is no need to rent an office or storage space.

They register the business at Companies House (£13 until recently, now £50) and apply for a free business bank account. They buy the website URL for a few quid, and then use a commercial website builder to get their product or service online within hours.

The total cost of getting started could be a tiny sum, less than £100. All the information, expertise and guidance they may ever need to be a success is freely available online. They use free social media accounts to spread the message. Within a week, they make their first sale. After a month, they are in profit. And whenever inspiration strikes, they can do it all again.

Costs may go up over time if they decide to advertise, bulk buy any raw materials they need, or use professional services, but that is within their control. It is not a barrier to getting going. The tools and technology are in place for Gen Z, and anyone else for that matter, to go their own way through solopreneurship or other small side hustles where they work with others.

These tools may feel more intuitive, reliable and trustworthy to a generation of digital natives that has grown up with an app-filled phone. Of course, it does not guarantee sufficient income to pay the bills. Starting up and scaling up have very different dynamics. The effort to get an enterprise off the ground does not indicate unstoppable momentum from that point onwards.

The Etsy- and Depop-type side hustles[1] have not just become more popular because they can be set up quickly and easily, but because they are *required* to pay the rent and the bills. This is not about wanting to be the next global household name or on the top 100 rich list. This is about supplementing an insufficient level of income from their main job to cover costs at modern levels.

If the side hustle start-up can become the scale up, or if a series of side hustles can generate a single income that pays the bills, then that is a great position to be in. For the most part, the reality is that Gen Z is not engaging with these activities because they believe it is only a

---

1   And many others too: Task Rabbit, Fiverr, Upwork.

matter of time before they make it big. They are doing it because one stream of income is not enough in today's world.

Pragmatism born of necessity

As with any generation, there are lots of examples of young, highly enterprising individuals making their mark, some of whom are phenomenally successful. Given the oldest Gen Z is not even 30 at the time of writing, it feels a little premature to judge if there are more than in any other generation. Having said that, I do expect this to be the case, particularly as traditional ways of working continue to erode.

A limited definition of 'entrepreneur' only referring to business moguls setting up multi-million multinational companies will also disintegrate. If you have an online business, you can be the modern equivalent of a multinational. The potential of selling online also means there will be more highly successful individuals than can ever be household names. In fact, we are already at that point.

There is an element of hedging bets or at least spreading the risk. One issue from the pandemic is that some professions and trades were hit far harder than others.[2] Although there was some general awareness of the risks of any pandemic, there was very little about which industries would be most affected. As we discovered in the UK, there was also a real limit on the quality of emergency planning by our national government. Gen Z has learned that life can be unpredictable and one source of income can also act as a single point of failure. If that disappears, they need another to rely on, and ideally more than one.

---

2 The Covid-19 pandemic had its own dynamic compared to its predecessors. Although the loss of life was colossal, the death rate across the global population was far smaller than the Spanish Flu a century earlier (0.09% vs 2.5%). It spread extremely quickly and approximately a third of cases were asymptomatic.

The same applied to 'casual' employment or those who had not worked long enough in an organisation to have a greater level of employment rights protecting their jobs. Those whose line of work could move to a remote model did so, but many could not. Some who worked in retail, hospitality and entertainment industries, for example, suffered badly, and all of these are typical jobs for young earners.

Gen Zers are making decisions about their professional futures in the context of an economic outlook that has remained problematic throughout their formative years. The oldest Millennials experienced a far higher rate of economic growth[vii] across their teenage years (3.4%) compared to the oldest Gen Z (2%). That 2% does not include the considerable dip in the aftermath of the Global Financial Crash, or the even more considerable dip as Covid-19 hit.

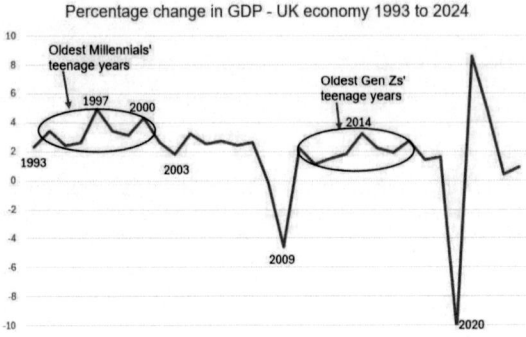

Figure 7: Percentage change in GDP – UK economy 1993 to 2024[viii]

The pandemic may have accentuated the difference, but it did not create it. The decision made by many Gen Zs to set up their own business has not been made with an expectation of a lucrative future, but of one where they are in a far weaker position than previous generations.

The freedom offered by going it alone should not be underestimated either, including in terms of controlling working hours and conditions.

Solopreneurs work when they want, where they want, for as long as they want. As you might expect, success will depend on how skilled and dedicated they are at making it happen. The internet, and social media in particular, is full of people and businesses not quite as busy or successful as they make out. That is also a pragmatic move. If you do not embellish your success, no one else will do it for you.

It is a more attractive alternative to what many have had in the workplace. Side hustles make part-time work a more viable option. The numbers who work part-time in the UK increased by 25% from 2000 to 2024.[ix] I spoke to a group of Gen Zs in one organisation where the large majority of them were part-time. The organisation did not need them to be full-time, and this gave them the freedom to pursue other interests. Some of these involved work with each other elsewhere. It is becoming increasingly common to have the same colleagues across different organisations.

For Boomers, Gen X and perhaps many Millennials, aiming to become an entrepreneur meant there was an intention of a future that was at the very least self-reliant, and ideally lucrative. Note the 'aiming'; the online tools were not there to guarantee that you would find the first rung of the ladder. Even the concept of solopreneurship needs to be separated from an expectation of automatic prosperity. Gen Zs are simply making a pragmatic response to the circumstances in front of them bequeathed to them by older generations. That starts with a pragmatic approach to survival.

In order to survive, let alone achieve any modicum of success, solopreneurs must be ultra reliable. They need to respond quickly to enquiries, ship products promptly and provide a high standard of customer service. They answer to themselves, not others. There is no HR department, sales team, front desk or head of finance.

The challenge for employers is how they can attract, and then retain, Gen Zers who are capable of building their own enterprises, but also talented enough to make a significant difference within an established organisation. From a pragmatic perspective, only a minority[x] of startups succeed. Putting all your eggs in one basket with a relatively low chance of success may not feel like a sensible move.

Employers who are content for employees to work only their contracted hours as the norm, or offer a little flexibility, can achieve the best of both worlds. They can attract talented employees who do a fantastic job within the contracted hours, whether on a full- or part-time basis. They can also have on the payroll employees building knowledge and skills from one or more side hustles, which could be invaluable for the organisation.

Either way, the Myth of Unreliable does not hold up. All too often when I meet with employers and they tell me their anecdotes, the conclusion I draw is that they appointed the wrong people. Most commonly they did so because the high-calibre candidates they sought were not attracted to them.

An apprehensive generation

There is no shortage of descriptions for the issues at the heart of the Myth of Unreliable. I had various options of what to call this particular characteristic. My research found references, some of them kinder than others, to Gen Z's lack of social confidence, tendency for risk aversion, guardedness and diffidence.

More than anything, there are also many references to mental health, and the types of comments that appear at the beginning of this chapter.

The word I have settled on for this key characteristic is 'apprehensive'. Initially, this referred to the end of the various lockdown periods during the pandemic, when life started to return to normal. However, in my view, it seems to have held up since then too, because the issues go beyond the pandemic. As was the case with economic circumstances, Covid amplified issues that were already present, or simply saw a trend continue.

In this section, I will cover the shocking statistics about the mental health of Gen Z, but also argue that, while challenging, they do not need to act as an insurmountable barrier to organisations recruiting and retaining as required.

The Prince's Trust has a fundraising scheme called The Class of Covid.[xi] It published research showing how the confidence of this generation dropped significantly during the pandemic. For example:

- 37% felt 'able to talk to senior people at work' before the pandemic, afterwards down to 21%.
- 68% said 'work was what they expected' before, now fallen to 49%.
- 40% 'lacked the confidence to make up their own minds' before, now up to 60%.

These are not small shifts, but the figures from prior to the pandemic do not reveal a position of strength either. What are the reasons for this?

Reputation management 24/7

A very significant factor is that Generation Z has had to deal with 24/7 reputation management from a very young age. This is particularly true for the older half, many of whom ended up with the earliest smartphones as the 'must-have gadget'. These were filled with social media data from apps that turned out to have unfathomable power, and in some short-lived cases[3] highly questionable morals.

All of this was beyond the imagination. More to the point, it was beyond the knowledge and experience of their parents and teachers, who were not able to guide children through the pitfalls they experienced simultaneously and in vast numbers. Other than the very real risks from adults posing as children, to name one example, they have also been filtering thousands of marketing messages every day at a speed no young person had to contemplate before the age of the smartphone.

Gen Xers, and our parents, used to talk about how many advertisements there might be on terrestrial television. Thinking back, in an age of four channels (and two of them had no advertisements), it was small fry compared to today. The same applied to radio where, although independent radio stations did exist, the advertisement-free BBC had a much greater market share of the nation's listening. Gen X also did not have to contend with a daily blizzard of misinformation or conspiracy theories. Politicians might have known that if you told someone the same message often enough, they might start to believe it, but the means of doing so were far more limited.

---

3   It could be justifiably argued that 'highly questionable morals' is a hallmark of some of the major social media platforms. Before the market settled with a relatively small number of high-profile platforms, there were many others, including some that vanished when law enforcement started to dig into them. In some cases, their lack of security contributed to some users using them for purposes other than which they had been designed. Around 10 years ago, I remember my jaw hitting the floor in a training session about those used to gain children's personal information, images and so on.

Given this, it is small wonder Gen Zers may take a little more time to build trust. This does not make them unreliable.

By the time I was running my second large secondary school in 2014, the issues were gaining momentum. The fear of an unwanted image or forgotten comment going viral and generating ridicule on a huge scale, and potentially for many years, was very real. Other fears were far more sinister and dangerous. The happy slap[xii] phenomenon may have felt like a high-level problem at the time in the mid-2000s, but it turned out to be only the start and a relatively innocent issue in retrospect. It was not a trend that individuals would want to capture for Instagram.

Social media impact

There is clear evidence that Gen Z does not have the same self-confidence as their predecessors. Surveys show that narcissism is down, thinking of yourself as above average is down, life satisfaction is down.

These are all reasons why Gen Z's cameras have become the ones turned off on the call. On top of that, they are data-protection conscious and also very aware of their digital imprint. This includes future implications from significant others and employers, both of whom may carry out their own background checks and neither of whom can be guaranteed to be transparent in doing so.

Gen Z has not just lived life through a screen, but through screens. They see more images of themselves and each other on camera, or through their icon images on social media, than anyone else. *The Truman Show* was released in 1998, six years before Facebook began; it is hard to look back at a film about an individual under the constant scrutiny of others in quite the same light. It now presents as a film where everyone bar one person has access to social media. More recent social media apps like Instagram, Snapchat and

WhatsApp give the user much more control over what others get to see. FaceTime and its equivalents are popular for calls with friends and family, and often more so than the old-fashioned telephone call. For the friends you have that you will never meet in person, which may be a significant proportion of friends for Gen Z, it's pretty important to know what they look like, not least to be confident they are who they say they are. As digital communication is all you have for the friends and work colleagues you will never meet, it may as well be as personal as possible.

As the Covid lockdowns ended, it was Gen Z who was back in the office first. There are several reasons for this. The first is that the physical workplace provides the kind of face-to-face interaction they want, and therefore opportunities for the soft skills many recognise they badly need to progress their careers. The cohort of Gen Zs who started their first adult jobs as the pandemic hit found themselves with work, but no workplace. Many found themselves with neither soon afterwards.

Working from home is far less advantageous where there is no designated workspace, let alone room, to work in. Even without the benefits of face-to-face interaction, a classroom is a much better environment to teach in compared to sitting on a bed with a laptop delivering to 30 students all day. Then there were the alternatives to desks and a place to rest your laptop such as ironing boards, piles of books and laundry baskets[xiii]. Sometimes there were two or more doing that in the same room. Living, working and sleeping in the same four walls day after day is not healthy.

The cumulative effect is significant. There are fewer physical workplaces and fewer romantic relationships too. Given the high proportion of couples[xiv] who would meet at work[4], there is a correlation between the two. It is also not the only reason for a reduction in romantic

---

4   There are different figures out there, but this survey says 45% .

relationships. The whole process of initiating a relationship for Gen Z is more loaded now, since it may be expected to be accompanied by Instagram posts or other social media content. To a lesser extent, this can also apply to friendships.

If you want to avoid ex-friends and ex-partners on social media, it is not easy. It is also very easy to be cut out of a conversation. The active WhatsApp group you are not in, which turned out to be a subgroup of the main group of friends, is just one example. The concept of FOMO[5] exists because there is so much more to miss out on. Beyond this lie the bittersweet algorithm-activated memories you receive of friends or relationships you used to have, or moments you now regret or cause you emotional pain. Automated, unwanted and painful nostalgia is not an issue Gen X had to deal with in their twenties. Gen Z has far more to deal with head on at a tender age.

The availability of dating apps has also created the impression that there may be a better fit out there. There is the idea that 'The One' is still worth searching for in 'next week's dates' but may never be found. For the apprehensive, a high-level commitment may also feel like a risk never worth taking. How 'perfect' does a match have to be before you know whether to proceed to a second or third date, let alone something as intimidating as a relationship? And for the workplace, how do you know whether you have found the best possible match in terms of industry and organisation, when so many other options are out there?

The sheer metrics of it all are frightening, not least the number of times phones are checked every day. After it gets to three figures, I suspect the researchers stop counting.[6] The number of posts, likes, impressions, views, clicks and comments are all tracked by every

---

5   Fear Of Missing Out. Where have you been if you didn't know that?

6   For a not-so-fictional account of this world, I strongly recommend
     Dave Eggers' dystopian novels *The Circle* and *The Every*.

platform everywhere. Depending on how much you want to get into it, so are steps, sleep quality, number of friends and so on.

None of this is new to members of Gen Z in the modern world, but they grew up with it in their formative and vulnerable years where character is shaped. It has never been more possible to know 'how you are doing' in so many areas of life that, decades ago, did not matter as much. These points of comparison do not always act as an aid to happiness. It can also lead to a reluctance to try something new in case of failure. Not only is failure more likely to be public, but if you fall over completely, its extent will also be revealed to compound the humiliation.

A risk-averse generation in a risk-managed world

Intellectual self-confidence amongst Gen Z is strong. In one survey, two-thirds judged they were higher than average. Given their academic record, this is not particularly surprising. The respondents to that survey were more positive about performance than social confidence, which was an even split. The perceived firepower is there to be used, if levels of confidence could be high enough to access it.

Confidence levels are not helped by a world that has become more risk-averse. I would argue that is a direct consequence of so much risk being designed out of life. Gen Z has grown up in a world where risk is far more likely to be identified and managed by specialists. As a result, they have come to expect that is the case, and that they do not have to make those judgements themselves.

I will name a couple of examples. When I speak at an event, I ask the audience if anyone got lost when finding the venue.[7] The answer is

---

7   Perhaps I should stress that this is about making a particular point on stage, rather than testing whether the directions sent out by the organiser were accurate.

always the same. It is nobody because they each have a device with all the information they need. The moving blue dot means you arrive in the right place and on time.

The second example is about attending events. Going to an arena or stadium concert is far removed from the experience of old. The chances of you losing your tickets in the months between purchase and the day itself are minimal. There is signage, and no shortage of people, for where you should go and security checks all along the way. Emergency routes, lockdown plans, toilets[8], traffic flow around the place are all managed.[9] Strategically placed barriers mitigate against anyone getting squished. The practice of crowd surfing is not only far less prevalent, but also greatly restricted.

Health and safety in the workplace and public realm are taken far more seriously, and managed more effectively, than was the case for previous generations. The reputation of an organisation depends on it, and images showing where it is not the case can go viral. This only accentuates the psychological impact of the biggest disasters, such as wars, a pandemic and financial crises, which are not averted despite all the available technology and knowledge.

This brings me to the topic that comes up over and over again by the leaders I work with: mental health, a subject at the root of the Snowflake Myth.

A 2019 survey of high-school-age students in the USA by *The Economist*[xv] showed almost three quarters considered 'anxiety and

---

8   Other than Wembley Arena, but let's not go there right now.
9   For an incredible example of where this didn't happen, look up the Fyre Festival from 2019. $100K for a ticket and attendees 'turned up to mattresses on rain-soaked floors, meals of cheese slices on bread and their luggage thrown into an unlit car park'.

depression' to be a major problem amongst people their age in their community. Almost no one said it was 'not a problem'. Bullying was considered a major issue by just over half, and topics like poverty and gangs just over a quarter.

I find this pretty shocking, not least because it is the year *before* the pandemic. Small wonder happiness is an issue amongst this generation.

On the basis of the Gen Z focus groups I hosted with young professionals, **I advise every manager at every level to take mental health seriously, be seen to do so and engage with the workforce along the way.** It is an absolute red line across the generation. Not taking it seriously will only lead to keeping the revolving door moving and unfortunate comments left on Glassdoor and other platforms for your future potential workforce to read.

One reason Gen Z is so adamant about the significance of mental health is because they see members of the older generation not talking about it and suffering as a result. This is particularly true in their families, where they see a lack of talking about their mental health leading to alcoholism, drug dependency or other health issues. In turn, these issues impacted their Gen Z childhood in the form of poor relationships with one or more parent at best and significant adverse childhood experiences at worst. The evidence that mental health concerns are not restricted to Gen Z backs them up.

There is a big gap to fill, not least for organisational and national productivity.

All social media's fault?

In March 2024, American social psychologist Jonathan Haidt published his book *The Anxious Generation*. In it, Haidt argues that social media and smartphone use have created a mental health crisis among Gen Z, particularly in their teenage years which then sustains beyond. He refers to the psychological damage from social media, including platforms that make little or no effort to restrict use to those they deem old enough to have an account. He details the developmental harm to its young users, as a 'phone-based childhood' leads to restricted cognitive growth.

The book is at its most jaw-dropping when Haidt talks about the rise in rates of depression, anxiety and suicide, which are particularly severe for adolescent girls. He has a potent argument for reimagining childhood in the modern age and a strong call to action for parents, school leaders and the tech companies themselves. Haidt is an advocate for unstructured childhood experiences and independent play, which encourages social development.

For the most part, I agree with what he has to say. I do not doubt the past and continuing impact of both the hardware and the software within a 'phone-based childhood', but I also argue that the issues driving the decline of Gen Z's mental health are broader than those identified in the book. He does not focus on Gen Z's poor financial situation, which means they are far less likely to be able to buy their own home, afford to have a family or retire. The same applies to the potential long-term impact of artificial intelligence, and the amplified sense of globalisation it complements. The causes of this anxiety are multi-faceted.

Haidt also does not focus on Gen Z's perspective on the climate crisis. A 2022 study stated that 59% of 16-25-year-olds were 'very' or 'extremely' worried about climate change.[xvi] In my experience, which has been accentuated by inaction from members of older generations in power. 'Climate anxiety' sees 'concern about climate change manifest as disturbing thoughts, overwhelming distress about future climate disasters and the continuing fate of humanity and the world. It can also translate into feelings of fear, insecurity, anger, exhaustion, powerlessness and sadness.[xvii]

I will focus on the impact of the finances in Chapters 6 in particular. At this stage, I will say that Gen Z's financial inheritance is not an accident and the implications, including for mental health, are very real. In my view, Haidt lets his peers off the hook.

The shift that Haidt identifies is not just about the advent of smartphones and their impact on the young, but also the creation of the digital native. Older generations had the opportunity to grow up in a world without smartphones. It was only in 2007[xviii] that the percentage of broadband users formed the majority, as the nation slowly (pun intended) switched over from the frustrations of a dial-up internet connection.

'Opportunity' might seem a strange description given what smartphones and broadband connections offer now, but digital natives have not had the opportunity to grow up in analogue without their every move and mistake being captured for posterity or the perpetual pressure of being permanently connected to anyone and anything. They have little reason or opportunity to be bored either, yet boredom also allows brains to decompress, problems to be unravelled and creative spaces to be found.

It can be difficult for an adolescent to understand what life was like only a couple of decades ago. Many adults will be familiar with a conversation that runs along the lines of 'so without phones or the internet, what did you do?' Those of my generation may forget that the same conversation happened in our childhoods as we wondered how life was bearable without a television.

Those who grew up without modern technology were excellent at creating their own experiences from very little as teenagers. Everyone will have their own version of this, but whether it was the patch of woodland to make dens, the playground at the rec that was the centre of all activity, or simply just being 'out' for hours with the same people in the same places, you had to use your imagination. The severe cuts to youth services[10] over time has also restricted opportunities for young people to develop their social skills.

On a more optimistic note, I do not see the impact of the phone growing ever worse. There is a generational element of this. The younger half of Gen Z have had parents with a decade's worth of experience with phones and social media. They understand the hardware and software, and the risks of both, much more deeply and are therefore able to parent more effectively. The challenges about a phone-based childhood remain, but a more informed set of adults does help to offset the risk.

Underprepared and unpractised

Gen Z's wider experiences have also been different from those in older generations, who were more likely in their formative years to:

- Work in a variety of jobs beyond school hours, university hours and during holidays.
- Spend time in the workplace with those from older generations.
- Have one or more work experience placements at school.

My approach to work experience placements while I was a headteacher might be seen as particularly old-fashioned. I have fond memories of bewildered students coming up to me holding their work

---

10   In my view, a broader set of youth services should be statutory, but this is a topic for another book.

experience letter telling me that there was no point in them spending a week in a bank, garage or garden centre. They would tell me "I don't want to do it when I am older and I won't like it, so there is no point." My standard reply would be something along the lines of: "In that case, you will learn exactly how long a working day is when you are bored doing something you don't want to do. Hopefully then you will work a lot harder on your return so you can get the qualifications you need to do something you do want to do." They did not appreciate it at the time, but they generally got it when they came back.[11]

I saw kids standing much taller on their return, and determined to work hard so they could open up their own opportunities. It was good for them to feel they had adults as colleagues and that they could develop the confidence to interact with them, rather than sitting behind desks staring at a screen.

Helicopter parenting

There are two recent trends worthy of some analysis, both published in 2024[12]. The first is a survey which reported that a quarter of parents of 22-year-olds were still tracking their children on their phones.[xix] The second is that a quarter of Gen Z parents were attending interviews with their child.[xx] That particular article went on to state that 'for those who had a parent come to an in-person interview, 37% say that their parent accompanied them to the office, 26% say their parent physically sat in the interview room and 7% that their parents

---

11   It was not done deliberately; ideally they had a good match and
      it was a positive experience for the employer as well. But I also
      believed in tough love, and helping kids make good decisions when
      they were adults.

12   Both sources are from the USA rather than the UK, but they make a
      point and I have had members of audiences report back on examples
      of the latter just in case you think it is too far-fetched to be true.

answered questions'. My question is not why the Gen Z brought the parent with them, assuming they had any choice, but why are the parents attending?

These similar examples are what has become known as helicopter parenting. If you are wondering what that phrase means, there are two key elements. One is being overprotective, because the parental 'helicopter' is constantly overhead hovering around their child. This could be in the form of the never-ending risk assessment, checking on productivity or ensuring they are avoiding any dangers. The other is about trying to have an excessive interest or involvement in their child's life to the extent that they go on to lack the resilience to handle the problems inevitably thrown at them down the line.

Examples of helicopter parenting include:

- An overemphasis on structure, rather than letting children create their own experiences in unstructured time. A child might have an endless series of after-school activities without a break, or strict restrictions on their free time.
- Hiring multiple tutors for a range of subjects, rather than insisting on the value of independent study skills.
- Excessive communication with their child's school, disputing what was said in class or requesting modifications to the curriculum or other teaching methods.[13]
- Insisting on accompanying their child on the journey to school, even in the teenage years, and not allowing journeys by foot or on bike.
- Intervening in conflicts between peers, rather than letting children resolve their own issues.

---

13   Do I have any experience in this? How long have you got? Actually, I didn't get unreasonable amounts of this and the Covid lockdown period made this trend considerably worse.

I do not want to overestimate the proportion of parents who engage in a helicopter style of this nature. I worked with hundreds of parents who would have enjoyed the luxury of spending more time with their kids or having the money to fund a broad range of experiences. However, for many, it is easier to book a series of extra-curricular activities, communicate with schools, and insist on arranging every playdate than once was the case. And plenty do. I am quite sure this has a negative impact on too many young people.

As I argue elsewhere, differences between generations are not as significant as differences within generations. The same applies to parents. It was very possible for previous generations of parents to be overprotective, and be too involved in their child's life before the technology was available to facilitate it further. An overprotective, over-involved approach to parenting can develop resilience as well as inhibit it. Children tend to have a strong sense of how they are parented compared to their peers, and resent a perceived lack of autonomy.

It is possible that there was always a proportion of parents who would have wanted to attend interviews with their child but now feel less inhibited doing so. The average age of a parent is higher than it has ever been, which means they have more life experience and a better idea of what can go wrong. This may also impact their approach to parenting. However, since I do not have evidence to go any further, this is a subject for another book.

Back to the point of tracking, and, indeed, the broader point. The Gen Xers who complain about those Gen Zers being accompanied at interviews or even at work are also their parents. The parents may not have developed the technology or social media platforms that left them at a loss as to how to respond (although let us not forget that some of them did), but they did have a significant impact on how their child spent their time and the extent to which they could make their own decisions. I come across leaders in the workplace who need a prompt to connect their experience as employers with their experience as parents. They can be far more accepting of challenge at home than they might be at work.

I can understand why parents would seek peace of mind and track their child on their phone, particularly as it gives the child more independence and safety when there is no one else at home after school. I also very much disagree with the idea that children are unsafe if they cannot be tracked. Ultimately, we need to guide children in making good decisions. Using technology for additional comfort blankets of safety may reduce the percentages of something going wrong, but it also creates a problem if young people do not learn to be independent.

It could be argued that there is a difference between having the facility to track someone and actively doing so all day. There is also a scale of independence, where it's not dependent or fully independent. There could be a middle ground where the buck does not have to stop with the young person for all their decisions. However, at what point should we stop using a parenting strategy that was custom in childhood, once the young person is in their late teens or twenties? Certainly, there are those who are unknowingly tracked, as well as those who are unknowingly tracking, because they have not removed the app. If a parent is still doing so when their child is in their early twenties, I would argue that the practice should have ceased some time ago, at the instigation of both parties. If a young professional has been old enough for some years to vote, join the military, drive a vehicle, travel abroad, start a business and get married, there is no need for their every movement to be monitored by their parents.

To an extent, the job interview example concerns me more. With phone tracking, a decision has to be made whether to stop or not.[14] With a job interview, there is an active decision to helicopter their child at a moment when their offspring needs to be seen to be sufficiently independent to get the job. Not only might it present itself as odd, but also counterproductive.

It is also revealing of other related practices about parents writing CVs, letters of application and undertaking research into prospective employers. If helicopter parenting is in place, the helicopter has to be put out of action at some point. Perhaps it is not just about minimising risk for their child, but also a realisation they have set up them up for a process where the young person is out of their depth because of the parents' own parenting style. There may even be a misconception that it protects their child's confidence for this to come to the surface while a parent is in the room so the latter can take the blame.

During my time as headteacher, this did happen on one occasion, although it was not intentional. A car parked outside my office, the candidate got out and entered reception with her mum, and then her mum left the building. The parking space outside my office may have looked like an obvious place to be out of the way, rather than being right next to the room where interviews would take place. Her face when she noticed her mum's car outside the window was a picture.

Since the candidate had travelled from Devon, it made sense that her mum gave her a lift and planned to spend some time in London during the day. This instance was never about a mother supporting her daughter through the selection process, but I might question a similar scenario today.[15]

---

14   It is possible that it could start at 22, or any age for that matter, but it is also unlikely.

15   Yes, she got the job and the location of the car broke the ice.

To return to Haidt, the smartphone may have created significant headaches for the modern parent, including those who want to avoid what can feel like an inevitable slide to a 'phone-based childhood'. There remains significant leeway in how those devices are used, and for how long, by both sides.

It is not just children that spend very significant time on their phones either. In 2023, the average adult in the UK spent 3 hours 50 minutes on their phones every day.[xxi] This was a reduction on the pandemic peak, but still approximately 30% higher than pre-pandemic 2019.

Not all about the phones

My view is that Haidt focuses on the impact of the smartphone too much to explain the decline in Gen Z's mental health. It was not the smartphone that created the issue of climate change, and has failed so significantly to act to prevent disaster. It is not the smartphone that caused the cost of living crisis, which has no sign of ending, and is leading many to the conclusion that they cannot afford to have children. It is also not the reason why so many Gen Zs may never be able to afford to retire.

Ironically, smartphones and associated technology have also created endless opportunities for information to be shared and acted upon, which could resolve all of the issues identified above if the members of older generations who run the large corporations or form governments chose to do so. The evidence so far is that few have a serious intention of changing.

In 2024, Australia's government proposed an amendment to the Online Safety Act for a minimum age of 16 on social media platforms. How this works, and how well it can be implemented in practice, will be closely watched around the world.

Strategies to support mental health

Below there is a range of strategies that organisations can use to support the mental health of their employees. I do not recommend it as a complete guide, nor portray myself as a health expert. For the most part, I am suggesting some general improvements to the company environment.

You need to take mental health seriously, be seen to take it seriously and model how you look after your own. You might not get it right all the time, but valuing mental health will take you a long way. External expertise on the subject is plentiful and can close the gap with your own knowledge and experience, as well as giving you confidence about the concessions you may not need to make.

Given this topic could be a book in itself, I have deliberately been selective in choosing strategies which have been raised with me in the course of my research.

1. Train your managers

Whatever you think about it, or knowledge you build, it will be the immediate line managers who have the most influence. They need to recognise the signs of mental health issues and understand what genuine empathy looks like.

2. Provide access to resources

Employee Assistance Programmes can be extremely good value, both for organisations and their employees. They need to be well-advertised and the benefits shared. Get those organisations in to provide workshops for staff and demonstrate it is a live partnership between you and them.

3. Financial literacy support

Available resources can include those relating to financial literacy and managing personal finances. It is very possible that more of your staff live hand to mouth than you might realise. Some adults can be spectacularly bad at dealing with their own money, whatever their level of income.

4. Adopt a hard line on working hours

Email signatures with words to the effect of 'I might contact you outside of working hours, but you do not need to reply' are common these days. I am no longer convinced they go far enough. Those messages can still generate notifications and restrict the benefits of a proper break between working days.

Work-based WhatsApp groups also need some restrictions about working practice. The same applies to office hours. Organisations that want to see their employees deliver their best quality also need to be strict about quantity. 'Right to disconnect' legislation in Australia gives employees a 'right to refuse to monitor, read or respond'[16] to 'contact from their employer'.[xxii] In practice, it would also be better if that contact was not made in the first place.

5. Focus on organisational culture

The culture of any organisation is determined by how the leaders and managers behave. I am diverting into my leadership team coaching work here, but too often the most important topics do not get airtime in the key strategic meetings. Everyone round the top table needs to be on the same page with this, and to have candid conversations when it is not in the right place.

---

16   There is a condition attached about whether contact is 'reasonable' or not, yet to be tested in the courts.

Strategies to be clear and thorough

"The companies that have the worst reputations do not develop them because they are rotten. It happens because they sell you a dream that's completely false."

Gen Zer

I cannot emphasise these enough: clarity and detail. **If you want to recruit, retain and motivate the best, you need to be ultra-clear. You also need to ensure that all the detail anyone may ever wish to see is easily accessible.** Clarity and detail collectively generate transparency, and that is the starting point for trust.

Gen Z has many good reasons to be suspicious of older generations. They include their financial inheritance and responsibility for resolving enormously expensive issues such as an ageing population and climate change.

Like everyone else, they are bombarded by content of all forms, and filtering out what is not useful, truthful or interesting absorbs a lot of energy. It also depends on having the experience and expertise to ignore, mute and block content that is malicious, exploitative or worse.

As an organisation, you cannot prevent your young staff members' exposure to the bombardment, but you can help your own case with the filtering. The most able Gen Zs are looking for organisations who get this right. It may be difficult to cut through and get attention amongst the noise, but organisations need to be seen to try.

In today's online climate, it is also a fine art to ensure that your website and job details are not only optimised to be found on search engines, but also to survive impact with the scanning eyes of a young professional processing information at high speed. Thousands of marketing messages are filtered out every day[17], so it is not easy to ensure that yours stops the scroll.

I would not advise any hiring manager to adopt a starting point that they may have to compromise on the quality of the candidates they seek to recruit. On the contrary, Gen Zs are looking for ambitious organisations who know what they are about and seek high-calibre candidates. All those coming out of university with first-class degrees did not put in the work to achieve them only to end up with an employer that's happy to put up with mediocre. If you want to attract the best, show that you are worth their time.

What do organisations need to be clear and detailed about?

At face value, there is a dichotomy between the need to be ultra-succinct so your details will be read, but also offering sufficient detail to create a strong sense of transparency. There will be a limit as to the number of words that can appear on your company website, or any promotional, induction or training materials, for example.

There is a big difference between giving the impression you are asking a potential candidate to read something, and ensuring it is available for them to read. A set of well-structured hyperlinks can go a long way, and by that I mean that the next level of detail is immediately obvious with further levels available as necessary. For example, a single link to company policies and procedures is helpful without an individual link to every last document within an intimidatingly long drop down menu.

---

17   This has obviously increased significantly over time, and blogs will quote anything between 4,000 to 10,000 per day without much evidence in terms of scientific study. In 10 years, it has gone from the low hundreds to many times that number. Even 3,000 per day is more than 1 million per year.

For good reasons, organisations may seek to protect the intellectual property of some of their documentation for those who are not yet employed. Gen Z will understand that, although they will also expect a straight answer to a question. Digital natives understand the value to organisations of every click and comment for the next wave of marketing (to follow), but will also protect their own interests.

Even better if your key documentation exists in a presentable format. Reassuring though it might be to see a 20-page document, short slide decks and videos can also go a long way. They will be useful in onboarding and training over time, as well as revisiting the material. Gen Z has a lot more experience with online training, at least as a proportion of their overall learning, than older generations. They are accustomed to well-laid-out programmes that flow and are easily navigable. Organisations need to meet the standard.

Organisations that have joined the B-Corp movement[xxiii] can cut through with today's young professionals, because the certification brings a guarantee that they 'meet high standards of social and environmental performance, transparency and accountability'. Young professionals have come to understand what this brand offers them.

At the time of writing, there are over two thousand B-Corps in the UK with 150,000 staff between them. Given the clarity offered by the certification, and the reputational damage it would cause if an organisation lost it, I expect these numbers to continue to grow quickly. Since the start of the pandemic, they have quadrupled already.[xxiv]

If you have not reviewed the small print for a while, go back to it and see what now needs to be in the 'big print'. Everyone understands the need for a little legalese, but not if it conceals something that should be front and centre.

Consider which questions applicants and new appointments have asked that were not easy for them to find. Better still, demonstrate some responsiveness by making clear that is what you have done. If a 'you said, we did' culture starts with those who send an application, it bodes well for the experience of the employee.

Examples include:

- Job description.
- Person specification.
- Hours of work.
- Flexibility, and the degree to which it may vary.
- Arrangements for leave.
- Benefits and perks.
- Training opportunities.
- Appraisal and feedback.
- Line management arrangements.
- Workplace culture.
- How employees can feed back.
- Last but not least... what the purpose of the work is.

I can hear HR managers sucking their teeth and saying that they do all of this already. Of course, this may well be true, but the point is how well and to what extent? The people who should be answering that question are not the HR team but the recent recruits.

It may feel clear and sufficiently detailed to someone who had a Saturday job as a teenager, one or more sets of work experience at school, a series of casual jobs in their late teens and early twenties, and then a number of employers and a whole series of workplaces before they reached their current levels. However, to prospective Gen Zs, it may well not satisfy their needs.

A procedural 'sign on every page' approach to HR lacks the feel and touch required to get the required buy-in from Gen Z. Person specifications are a good example. They can stay the same for years, untouched let alone reviewed. Their relationship with the recruitment process, and the job itself, may be tenuous. A person specification needs to live and breathe what you want and expect from employees, and therefore what they can expect from their colleagues. If employees require development in specific areas, you need resources on hand to support them in addressing it. Person specifications can also be too long; a 'less is more' approach offers a greater degree of clarity.

There is also an argument that organisations need to be more selective in what they are really looking for in all of knowledge, expertise, skills and personal characteristics in order to recruit. Given the imbalance in supply and demand, and the recruitment difficulties for so many organisations, this presents as counterintuitive. Yet a 'catch all' model of marketing no longer holds water. Organisations have a higher chance of appealing to those they really want and need by taking the risk of putting off many potential candidates. In this day and age, you need to be more 'Marmite' in order to stand out. Retention figures rise in the long term when the right people take notice of the advertisement.

There is clearly a very considerable issue about the steeply rising numbers of young adults who are not in education, employment or training. Shockingly, the numbers grew by approximately a third between 2021 and 2024.[xxv] Since that point, the number has reached a million young people.

This problem is much wider than Gen Z. In 2024, 11 million[xxvi] working-age people (16-64) did not have a paid job, of which 9.3 million were not actively looking. The UK has more people out of its workforce than it did during the pandemic. The historically low total of 1.5 million unemployed (a third of whom are aged 16-24) masks the true nature of the issue.

I am going to discount the two million 16-24 aged students from the figures. Over a million 50-64 had retired, although the 1.5+ million of over 65s still in the workplace compensates for this.

The more significant issues for the older age groups are:

- 2.4 million are 'sick'.
- 1.5 million are carers, perhaps for young children where the cost of childcare is prohibitive or for older generations where the same applies.
- 0.75 million are 'other', which I assume covers a range of issues.

For 16-24-year-olds, the 1 million 'inactives' are made up of approximately 500,000 unemployed, 250,000 sick, a further 250,000 caring and almost 100,000 'other'. While there is clearly an issue with health, including mental health, among Gen Z, they represent approximately 10% of those not well enough to work.

Employers do comment on not being able to find the skills they want. More often, I hear, from both employers and employees, that Gen Z often do not feel 'adequately equipped' for the workplace.[xxvii]

It is much better for employers to work out what matters most from the person specification, and determine the one or two most prized skills or knowledge base when recruiting. The rest you can train or develop over time. Even if it is not the position an employer may prefer to find themselves in, it also makes for a simpler search and recruitment process. For a prospective employee, it may generate more reassurance than you might ever imagine. The realisation that they do not have to tick every single box on the job description and person specification to a high standard, as they had to do to achieve top grades in their examinations, will make a difference to the volume and quality of applications.

Where else can you be clear and through? Examples include:

- How line management and appraisal operate, including the frequency of a sit-down, in-person meeting where practicable
- What a typical day might look like
- What an employee should check with their manager before acting
- The relationship that an employee may have with their manager's manager

Your current employees will have the best answers for how your specific organisation can be clear and thorough.

Strategies to supply resources

The quality and nature of your documentation forms a window through which you will be seen and judged by Gen Z, so make sure it is available in varied formats and of high quality. Churning out unaltered versions of resources year after year will only be to your detriment.

Gen Z's education, and their early professional life, has taught them that the resources on offer to help with their revision are vast and available in any format they choose. A choice of step-by-step guides are instantly available for everything, and these assume no prior knowledge. Furthermore, the standard of tools available to schools has skyrocketed in recent years, and the same applies to online course providers, so Gen Z is used to high quality of resources as well as availability. Resources should cross-reference and link to anything that could possibly be of use to anyone.

Video resources have a further advantage in this day and age, in that they convey a greater degree of authenticity. This has particular relevance for those engaged in recruitment processes, or marketing their organisation in general. Anyone can piece words together and make a claim. The same can apply to video too, of course, but it is harder to do so and arguably easier to spot once you have seen a few of these things. The reputational risks for an organisation caught faking videos used in job adverts are considerable, given the propensity for them to go viral and live at the top of a Google search.

Video testimonials from your current employees on your website will add a lot more credibility than an image and a grab quote. It is at least as important to have the same from decision-makers and those who run the company. It gives prospective employees the opportunity to judge if they are trustworthy and genuine, and current employees the opportunity to compare if what they were told at the outset matches reality.

A short video, posted on TikTok and Instagram as well as the company website and job boards, about a job and what an employer is looking for can go a long way. At least it shows you are trying, and the feedback you will get informs the next one.

As employers, you need to make sure your job role documentation is crystal clear and represents what you really want and need. If you need employees to undertake tasks for which they may not be best suited or could be automated elsewhere, explain why. Gen Z understands the need for efficiency, so if something presents as inefficient at face value, be clear on the value you see it adding.

The same applies to application forms. How difficult is it to apply to work at your organisation? Mobile-optimised forms can take minutes to complete, and enable the same CV and related documentation to be sent to multiple people. Making this option available can make a significant difference to the depth and quality of your field. For your prospective employees, the application process forms a portal into what it is truly like to work with you.

If you are already used to working with Applicant Tracking Systems (ATS), whether your own or from elsewhere, you may be mystified as to how others are not in the same position or how you would manage without one.[18] Small and medium-sized organisations are much less likely to have an ATS. Within them lies a myriad of user-unfriendly Word documents and clunky PDFs that lead to eye-rolls and disengagement by quality candidates.

I would also ask organisations whether they really need candidates to complete every part of the application process in advance, particularly if they are struggling to recruit or part of an industry in the same position. It may be your preference that each candidate writes a brand new two-page letter of application so you can see their writing skills, and perhaps your advertised role is so attractive that you will receive them.

You may also receive more AI-generated unreadable garbage than you might have ever dreamed was possible. Worse than that, you put off the calibre of candidate you want to attract and never get to find out. Young candidates will understand why communication skills are important, particularly if you give an explanation, but may also expect you to test them during an interview process, rather than through the application. They will also expect that you are open to using AI to streamline writing activities rather than always starting with a blank page.

---

18   In the USA, over 70% of large companies have an ATS, but only
      20% of small to medium-sized.

Gen Z will also expect that you take and act upon feedback from your employees, not least because they assume you want to improve as an organisation. And if you don't, why would they stay and encourage others to arrive?

Demonstrating you are clear and thorough also indicates you prioritise getting the detail right. This brings one other major advantage. It generates confidence that your company is more likely to survive whenever the next apparently unforeseeable economic crash, pandemic or political crisis hits. Gen Z has become very familiar with the unpredictability of life, arguably more so than either Millennials or Gen X. They value those from the older generations who think ahead.

Even better if you do not just think ahead but demonstrate doing so to your employees. Smart organisations need to be clear and thorough about being clear and thorough. Retaining staff is not just about showing clear progression routes, pay and benefits, or sticking to your values. It is about showing that you are securing the long-term future of the organisation, and listening to your workforce along the way.

Strategies to adopt flexibility

From the Deloitte 2021[xxviii] survey, flexibility stands out as important and is a distance ahead of other factors when it comes to Gen Z appeal. Even so, I would like to put this in a little perspective.

First of all, in 2021, flexibility may have had a higher level of significance than will prove to be the case in the future. That said, it is still the most critical behaviour to Gen Z, Millennials not rating it as crucial to the same degree. Now, flexibility may be important, but you do not have to be flexible to the extent that it harms your organisation. You may not need to be more flexible than you feel truly comfortable with either.

What is important is that you are clear and consistent around how flexible you are prepared to be and how you came to that decision. While employees expect employers to make decisions, they also expect some consultation along the way. Flexibility does not mean there are no rules, or that you are no longer in charge. You might lose people if you do not give them what they want, but if you are clear about your rationale and what you will lose if you go further, stick with your decision.

Unreliability among Gen Z is a myth. At least, what we see as their desire to 'opt out' is justifiable. It is a pragmatic response to their circumstances and apprehension born out of their upbringing. With the right strategies to communicate and support them, it is possible to provide working conditions that help Gen Z not only thrive, but stay and grow in your organisation.

Endnotes

i   *Etsy: number of active buyers 2023 | Statista.* (2024, October 14). Statista. https://www.statista.com/statistics/409375/etsy-active-buyers/

ii   Printful (2024) *11 Interesting Etsy Statistics You Need to Know in 2024.* https://www.printful.com/uk/blog/etsy-statistics?srsltid=Afm BOoras6XRWJFLM7iuYM3DQ8kFkUNxxqFqChK5W1H6EQhDhc 2CEsRX

iii   *Companies register activities April 2023 to March 2024.* (2024, November 28). GOV.UK. https://www.gov.uk/government/statistics/companies-register-activities-statistical-release-april-2023-to-march-2024/companies-register-activities-april-2023-to-march-2024

iv   *Companies register activities April 2023 to March 2024.* (2024, November 28). GOV.UK. https://www.gov.uk/government/statistics/companies-register-activities-statistical-release-april-2023-to-march-2024/companies-register-activities-april-2023-to-march-2024

v   *Santander shortlists 100 UK start-ups for its 2024 awards competition | Santander UK.* (2024, September 9). https://www.santander.co.uk/about-santander/media-centre/press-releases/santander-shortlists-100-uk-start-ups-for-its-2024

vi   Pardo, S. B., & Pardo, S. B. (2023, January 18). Survey shows majority of Gen Z aspire to be their own boss. *International Accounting Bulletin.* https://www.internationalaccountingbulletin.com/news/survey-shows-majority-of-gen-z-aspire-to-be-their-own-boss/

vii   *Gross Domestic Product: Year on Year growth: CVM SA % – Office for National Statistics.* (2025, February 13). https://www.ons.gov.uk/economy/grossdomesticproductgdp/timeseries/ihyp/pn2

viii   *Gross Domestic Product: Quarter on Quarter growth: CVM SA % – Office for National Statistics.* (2025, February 13). https://www.ons.gov.uk/economy/grossdomesticproductgdp/timeseries/ihyq/pn2

ix   Statista. (2025, March 13). *Number of part-time workers in the UK 2000-2024.* https://www.statista.com/statistics/621607/number-of-part-time-workers-in-the-uk/

x   Jones, S., & Jones, S. (2023, October 9). *How many businesses fail in the first year in the UK? Business Insolvency Helpline.* https://business-insolvency-helpline.co.uk/how-many-businesses-fail-in-the-first-year-in-the-uk/#:~:text=According%20to%20data%20from%20Startup,culture%20and%20access%20to%20capital.

xi   *The Class of Covid | How we can help | The King's Trust.* (n.d.). https://www.princes-trust.org.uk/help-for-young-people/the-class-of-covid

xii   Harrison, A., & Harrison, A. (2024, July 27). *A complete history of Happy-Slapping.* VICE. https://www.vice.com/en/article/a-complete-history-of-happy-slapping/

xiii   Scully, E. (2020, March 16). Office workers share their VERY imaginative working from home set ups. *Mail Online.* https://www.dailymail.co.uk/femail/article-8116385/Office-workers-share-imaginative-working-home-set-ups.html

xiv   Editorial Team (2024) *45% of people have met a substantial partner in the office,* HR News. https://hrnews.co.uk/45-of-people-have-met-a-substantial-partner-in-the-office/

xv   The Economist. (2019, February 27). Generation Z is stressed, depressed and exam-obsessed. *The Economist.* https://www.economist.com/graphic-detail/2019/02/27/generation-z-is-stressed-depressed-and-exam-obsessed

xvi   Windsor-Shellard, C. B. K. E. a. B. (2022, October 27). *Worries about climate change, Great Britain* – Office for National Statistics. https://www.ons.gov.uk/peoplepopulationandcommunity/wellbeing/articles/worriesaboutclimatechangegreatbritain/septembertooctober2022

xvii   *Gen Z's climate anxiety is real and needs action -- for everyone's wellbeing.* (2024, March 24). ScienceDaily. https://www.sciencedaily.com/releases/2024/03/240305134319.htm#:~:text=It%20can%20also%20translate%20into,could%20have%20major%20future%20ramifications

xviii   Plusnet. (n.d.). *History of the Internet | When was the Internet invented? | Plusnet.* https://www.plus.net/broadband/discover/history-of-the-internet/#:~:text=Broadband%20first%20started%20to%20replace,Asymmetric%20Digital%20Subscriber%20Line)%20connection.

xix   Cavendish, C. (2024, February 17). Why having a Gen Z child means parenting an adult. *Financial Times*. https://www.ft.com/content/3c820604-5153-4f24-8645-179371eca039

xx   *1 in 4 Gen Zers Brought a Parent to a Job Interview – ResumeTemplates.com*. (2024, September 6). ResumeTemplates.com. https://www.resumetemplates.com/1-in-4-gen-zers-brought-a-parent-to-a-job-interview/

xxi   Statista. (2024, May 10). *UK: daily hours spent on mobile 2019-2023*. https://www.statista.com/statistics/1285042/uk-daily-time-spent-mobile-usage/#:~:text=In%202023%2C%20users%20in%20the,of%20the%20COVID%2D19%20pandemic

xxii   *Right to disconnect – Fair Work Ombudsman*. (n.d.-b). https://www.fairwork.gov.au/employment-conditions/hours-of-work-breaks-and-rosters/right-to-disconnect

xxiii   *The UK B Corporation movement*. (n.d.). B Lab UK. https://bcorporation.uk/

xxiv   Lane, E. (2024, April 16). *Benefits and barriers to B Corp certification*. Energise. https://www.energise.com/benefits-barriers-b-corp-certification/

xxv   Brand, A. (2024, August 27). *Rising number of young people not in education or work hits 872,000, new data reveals*. HRreview. https://hrreview.co.uk/hr-news/future-of-work-hr-news/rising-number-of-young-people-not-in-education-or-work-hits-872000-new-data-reveals/376453

xxvi   Georgieva, R. C. &. G. (2024, November 26). *Who are the millions of Britons not working, and why?* BBC News. https://www.bbc.co.uk/news/business-52660591

xxvii   Team, G. R. (2024, March 23). *Addressing the Gen Z skills gap*. FDM Group. https://www.fdmgroup.com/news-insights/gen-z-skills-gap/

xxviii Deloitte. (2021). A call for accountability and action. In *THE DELOITTE GLOBAL 2021 MILLENNIAL AND GEN Z SURVEY*. https://www2.deloitte.com/content/dam/Deloitte/mk/Documents/about-deloitte/2021-deloitte-global-millennial-survey-report.pdf

5

The Myth of Instant

"The trouble with young professionals these days is that they expect to find themselves promoted before they have learned anything. You have to start at the bottom because that's how much you know. It doesn't happen overnight. It takes years and years to be ready to move up. When you are ready, you will be told."

Career 'guidance' given to me in the mid-90s

The pace of modern life appears to become ever faster. Expectations of what can be achieved in no time at all, with multiple updates along the way, are unrecognisable from not so many years ago.

Booking a holiday is a good example. Decades ago, January would see one holiday catalogue after another arriving through the door. Selecting where to go involved paper-based research, watching travel shows on TV and, if you were really committed, scrolling through Teletext.[1] Even though it was possible to buy a holiday by phone, and risk reading out your credit card number to a room full of people, many did not. They went to their nearest travel agent, sat down with a person and considered the options. In short, it was a morning's work, give or take. Even then, the prospect of seeing what your accommodation might look like, and understanding what you were getting for your money, was slim. That was left as a surprise for when you got there.

Then there's communications in general. Remember my network manager colleague who made use of the pigeon hole system to share messages across the school? While those pigeon holes were full of unopened envelopes, scrap paper and unread memos, that was all we had. There were no smartphones, Gmail or WhatsApp. The days before email were so different to today.

In my first senior job, I remember seeing the headteacher walking back to his office holding an empty wire tray that he had just spent five hours dealing with, only to be greeted with another in its place full to the brim. With email, we are all that headteacher all of the time. Communication is constant, as are the expectations of instantaneous response.

---

1   I am claiming some expertise on this, and not because of the holidays I worked on. I spent one long summer break from university selling holidays over the phone. Those who called had either gone to the relevant page on Teletext, or had been watching TV in the small hours when there were no programmes other than a series of pages with holiday details. This often meant that key decisions were made in the early hours of the morning and under the influence. Oh, you want to know what Teletext was? Essentially information pages with hideous graphics on both the BBC and ITV service. It was seriously helpful at the time if news and sport were your thing and if you had a job selling holidays over the phone.

Want to do your Christmas shopping without leaving the house? Instantly done. Find a builder, window cleaner, architect or plumber? The search is over in seconds. The second you post your request on the online platform, your phone will start to ring. Don't fancy cooking? Your local takeaway or dark kitchen[2] will get you whatever you want at any time and you can track the moped bringing it. You get the picture.

It has become second nature to have multiple windows open, have a variety of devices carrying out different functions within reach, and Gen Z has grown up with that. If a product is ordered online, not only is the process over in seconds, but you can track it to your door with an ever shorter window in which it will arrive so you can plan your time around it. In the UK at least, the length of time from order to home delivery is unbelievably quick. We used to think 28 days for delivery was good enough, now 28 hours is more than feasible, as is 28 minutes for the takeaway.

The Myth of Instant focuses on the concept that Gen Z expects everything quickly all of the time. Along with this is the idea that patience is not a virtue they possess, not least because systems have been designed to mean patience is no longer necessary.

In this chapter, I will argue that patience is a stand-out characteristic of Gen Z. While it does not apply to everything, Gen Z is far from the only generation to expect high levels of pace and responsiveness. We have all got used to modern technology enabling faster productivity in our personal and professional lives, but there are some areas where

---

2   A dark kitchen is a commercial kitchen that prepares food exclusively for delivery only. They don't have restaurants with seating for customers. Dark kitchen appears to be the most popular term, but virtual, cloud and ghost kitchens are alternatives. This is how you manage to get Wagamama food when there isn't a branch around you for many miles.

Gen Z have been forced to wait and accept delayed gratification. Later in the chapter, I will cover employers' responsiveness in the workplace and the key strategy of giving feedback at work.

Workplace observations

These are examples of what I hear from my peers and in the media.

- "They want promotion so quickly, and then expect the next one. They do not understand why it takes years to build the experience necessary to move up a level. They want a checklist to progress through and expect that to be all they ever need."
- "When they send a message or email, they expect a reply so quickly. It is not that simple. Too often those messages ask me for something they could and should find themselves. They do not like that answer when I give it. I am their manager, not a general help desk."
- "Some problems are complex, and our job is to solve them. Complex problems take time to work through, and they can change along the way. If instant solutions were available, we would use them, and I would not have needed to hire new young staff to help me."
- "When the technology goes down, like a power cut or internet outage, they have no idea what to do. We have all become reliant on technology, but you do not need it for everything. White boards, pens and Post-it notes can be more effective. When we are properly together, there can be real benefits."
- "They ask me for feedback on their performance far more often than is reasonable, and also more than is productive. They want to know instantly how they have done on every single thing, and can really struggle if they do not get the affirmation they are looking for."
- "They can be very averse to detail. I am asked for a short

summary on a report that might only be 10 pages long. Not everything can be condensed, and I'm not prepared to use AI to make it happen. I need them to value the broader picture."

- "They have an expectation of live updates about company performance. There are some aspects of that I cannot quantify, and also examples where I am not at liberty to explain why either. They need to accept that more than some of them do."

- "Sometimes work is messy. Issues might get worse rather than better when you first address them, which they find difficult to contemplate. I need staff who embrace that messiness and want to find a way through it, not those who flinch at the first sign of something going backwards."

- "They want to know how they are doing about everything all of the time. I do not have the time to tell them. We have structures and processes in place for that."

- "There is no patience about anything. If I agree to a flexible work request, they expect it to be implemented instantly. They do not understand why it might take months to put into place. The same applies when I agree to suggestions about how the workplace can be improved. I wish I had a magic wand, but I do not."

A patient generation

"There's a lack of certainty. We've lived through unprecedented times for about a decade, from Trump to Brexit, five prime ministers in six years, a global pandemic, then you start working and there's a recession on the horizon. It is a bunch of random events and the future is not as it might have been."

Gen Zer

The longer we have lived with the world wide web, the more it feels as though we have barely scratched the surface with its possibilities. Search engines have reduced the time required to research a topic from many hours to a matter of seconds. It might take some minutes to work out which sources you can rely upon, then synthesise them into something meaningful, but the legwork is no longer a factor. If a source is not in your chosen language or was published abroad, that is no longer a barrier either.

Online banking has allowed its users to complete complex financial transactions in minutes that would have previously required hours of in-person bank visits, including transferring funds, paying bills, and managing investments. The queues alone were enough to put people off in years gone by.

Given all this, you would be forgiven for thinking Gen Zers are impatient because life has sped up. Yet, there are also ways in which life has slowed down in recent years, particularly for Generation Z, resulting in them having to delay certain milestones or meaningful activities. Could this have made them more patient as a generation? This is the focus of this section.

Virtual but not reality

By young adulthood, Gen Z has been exposed to far more experiences online than was the case for the previous generation, particularly those whose teenage years preceded the digital revolution. Yet there is a dissonance between this and what is experienced in real life. Frequently this is because awareness of risks often means a delay in actions.

I will not repeat all the details here about Gen Z's tendency to be well-behaved from the Myth of Lazy. As a reminder, I will say that Gen Z has experimented less with drugs and alcohol, and had fewer sexual relationships. On average, members of this generation have also waited longer for their first such relationship, as well as their first alcoholic drink.[i] In addition, as mentioned in the Myth of Unreliable, a lot of risk has been engineered out of life. The safety features and general reliability of modern cars, for example, mean that people are less likely to drive one that breaks down or is involved in a collision. Their door cams and alarm systems protect them from break-ins and act as a deterrent for other crimes. The convenience afforded by modern technology means you can arrive just on time for a bus and are less likely to lose your train tickets. Just in case you forget what you are supposed to do and when, a series of emails and notifications will arrive in the preceding days, hours or minutes to minimise the possibility of missing a delivery or not having a QR code to hand. Today's 'done-for-you' culture means that you do not have to think about a whole range of tasks, while being simultaneously hyperaware.

The endless presence of the camera has regulated behaviour and extensive research about how to do pretty much anything is available in text and video form. A lower possibility of mistakes has also meant there are fewer opportunities to learn from them, or expect that you may have to make a few first before you start to get it right.

As discussed elsewhere in this book, parenting styles may also have mitigated against children making necessary mistakes. A risk-free childhood is no preparation for adulthood. It limits exposure to unplanned yet memorable experiences, such as getting lost, bumping into an old friend you had lost contact with or making up your own fun. Thinking on your feet and working something out generates confidence. Even glorious failures provide something to celebrate down the line because you tried and learned along the way.

Patient but not by choice

The average age of marriage continues to rise. In 2018, the average age for newlyweds was closer to 40 than 30 (being 38 for men and 36 for women, including marriages beyond an individual's first. For first marriages it is 31, up from 23 in 1970). When they were first marrying,, many Boomers got married so they could move out of home and get their own place. It feels ironic that there are fewer social and cultural barriers to the former, but very significant financial barriers to the latter in today's world. These include the cost of renting or owning, as well as the cost of the wedding.

The graph below shows that the number of marriages per year has fallen by half since the early 1970s and a third since the late 1980s.[3]

Figure 8 – Number of marriages that took place each year 1970 to 2019, England and Wales[ii]

The average age of becoming a parent has also risen over time. As the youngest Gen Z was born in 2012, we will be waiting a while to find out how this pans out over the course of this generation, but it would be a surprise if it declined.

---

3   Interestingly the divorce trend line continued to climb until the early nineties, despite the reduced number of marriages. This graph stops at 2019 as the Covid lockdown meant it was harder to get married in 2020, and perhaps less appealing given the financial pressures of the time. Also interestingly the number of marriages may have fallen by two thirds in 2019, but the divorce rate barely skipped a beat.

The age of parenthood for women has gone up from just over 26 in 1995 to almost 31 in 2024.[iii] Five additional years is a long time as a proportion of adult life. This may also reflect the nature of an informed, pragmatic generation, since part of this rise results from a decline in teenage pregnancies.

Not only are parenthood and marriage delayed, but so too is the prospect of moving out or owning property. Over time, the evidence is likely to show that the pandemic has accentuated all three, as seen here.

In addition to this are the rises in retirement and state pension ages, and the steep decline of the private sector pension. The table below illustrates the former. The possibilities of a state pension age of at least 70 seems realistic for Gen Z, and possibly Millennials too.

This is unfortunately accompanied by slower gains in life expectancy. Average life expectancy rose by eight years for males (71 to 79) and six years for females (77 to 83) 1980 to 2010. Neither figure has budged since. The expansion of the number of years spent working can only be at the cost of the number of years spent in retirement.

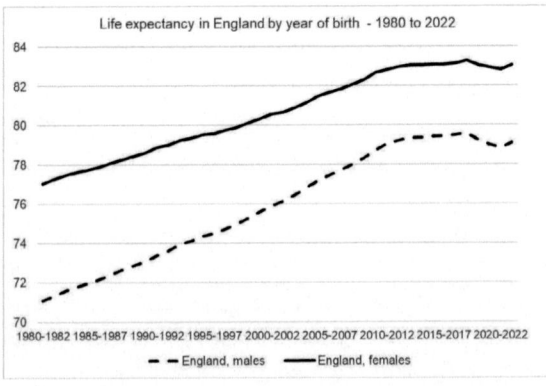

Figure 9: Life expectancy in the UK over time in England 1980 to 2023[iv]

For those who can never afford to retire, this may also be accompanied by a steep decline in living standards or a growth in the number of multi-generational households. The future trend may not just be those who can never afford to leave home until comparatively late in life, but also parents moving in with their adult children so they can afford to stop working by sharing the cost of rent and utilities.

In short, Generation Z can expect to be working for a much longer period of time and not out of choice. This lack of choice is accompanied by a loss of control, as exemplified by the quote at the start of this chapter.

The significance of levels of frustration about Deliveroo or an Uber taxi arriving 10 minutes later than scheduled, or having to wait an extra year for promotion, pales against never buying property, marrying, parenting or retiring.

A less linear life

The traditional linear route of education to work to retirement now has many alternatives. It is possible to be in two or more of those phases at the same time, and move backwards and forwards. University courses can begin at any point of adult life and work exists in many forms beyond the 9 to 5 Monday to Friday.

Although individuals may have a choice in theory to retire when they like, return to full-time study, or choose a job they love with a lower salary or more flexible options, these are luxuries not open to everyone. Gen Z knows full well the choices that exist for others, but without a sense they may apply to them. Even striving harder, sooner and for longer than older generations does not guarantee they will get there.

A lack of financial stability and certainty are key drivers of behaviour for Gen Z. Given the length of time they are likely to have to work, and the lack of retirement years at the other end, why rush if their circumstances mean it is not necessary to do so? Similarly, why rush to find your career of choice if there are other opportunities along the way?

Gen Z's propensity for patience should not be underrated. Much of it may not have been wanted on their behalf, but for employers who are able to show what the future will look like for their employees, there is also much to build upon if accompanied by the stability and certainty they desire.

Managers who extrapolate Gen Z's expectations of carrying out tasks quickly and efficiently online to how they run their whole lives risk causing offence. Telling your own stories about the difficulties of saving a 5% deposit to get on the housing ladder at 25 when property was far less expensive will not endear you to them.

I have heard my peers say words to this effect: "If Gen Z could cut out their coffee shop habits, they would be able to afford to buy a property." In 2023, the average 'first time buyer property price' was £240,000, and the average deposit was approximately 15% or £34,500[v]. The average price of a takeaway coffee is currently[vi] (and conveniently for mathematical purposes) £3.40. Therefore, 10,000 coffees get you the deposit you might require, assuming that 15% deposits are still available by the time you have got that far. It takes over 40 years of buying one coffee five times per week to save that amount of money.

Other areas of spending could be examined too, but that is not really the point. At the time of writing, the average net monthly income is £2,297 and average monthly rent paid in the UK is £1,307[4], over

---

4   Almost 400 of those coffees.

50% for a single earner and over a quarter if shared between two. Rent inflation has been almost 1% higher on average than the general level since 1989.[vii] That compound interest makes a vast difference over time[5]. The number of people renting has increased by over 50% in 30 years (from approximately 6 million in 1993 to 9.5 million in 2023). The price of rent, let alone all other bills, makes it much harder for Gen Z ever to own a property.

It is not the case that Gen Z universally wants to put down roots and start a family. For some I have spoken to, there is a sense of 'what you never had, you never miss'. This does not take away from the monthly struggle to meet the cost of living, particularly if renting, a sense that their personal lives may not progress for some time and that choices are restricted.

No manager or leader can counter the financial pressures of all their existing and future Gen Z staff. Understanding the issue can at least generate some empathy and inform your practice. There are some ways in which expectations can be managed, and practices changed where necessary. For that, I am going to focus on employee performance.

Strategies to involve employees in regular feedback

"I ask my managers how they think I am doing, and how I could improve, but I rarely get an answer. It doesn't matter whether I pass them in the corridor or send them an email. What is wrong with asking how I could be better? I'm told that I need to wait for appraisal, but that's months away. Do they not want me to improve?"

Gen Zer

---

5   An additional 1% per year makes approximately 40% difference across 35 years.

"Every time I pass them in the corridor I am being asked how I think they are doing, and what they could do better. I get emails from them too, directly, asking me the same kind of questions. If I answer them, it appears to be taken as some form of invitation to keep asking (and asking). Why can't our younger staff go with the same appraisal system we have for everyone else? It works! Doesn't it?"

Gen X manager

Managing performance is a key aspect of any leader's role, especially needed for engagement. I have heard many similar stories from leaders to the one above. Their professional experience is that meetings or discussions about performance are typically sporadic affairs.

Consequently, the whole concept of 'engagement' can leave leaders feeling a little lost. An annual staff questionnaire, a single meeting to review progress and set targets, a wooden suggestion box on the reception desk and a Christmas party used to be all that was required.

Gen Z has been taught to have very different expectations around engagement. They do not anticipate their ideas will disappear into the ether. They expect to have a voice. This section will focus on the value of giving regular and precise feedback, but the detail will cover wider aspects around engagement.

The first point to note is that we are living in the age of feedback. There really is no shortage. At any particular time, an individual may have access to automated feedback from:

- Social media (number of connections/followers/friends, number of impressions/likes/hearts/comments).

- Online learning (progression statistics through a course, test scores on individual modules).
- Health (steps in particular but also, for those with Fitbit and the like, heart rate, calories, sleep quality/quantity).
- Financial budgeting (how much has been spent in each category, and the value of ISAs or other funds).

Then there is time tracking, energy consumption, and monitoring 'streaks' (on apps like Duolingo[6], Wordle and so on) among many other possibilities. The key is not just the quantity and range of metrics; it is that they are instantly available and often updated by the second. A personal life dashboard is not for me, but I am probably closer to it than I admit.

Professional life cannot work in the same way, or at least not healthily. It is not attractive when it does. That is not to say the metrics are a bad thing, but quantitative data has its limits. If a workplace is merely one long fulfilment centre, there will be limitations to any recruitment and retention strategy. Values, ethos, culture all matter considerably to Gen Z, perhaps not least because they do not fit into a dashboard methodology. Gen Z understands very well the need to measure, but not above all else.

Appraisal involvement

Appraisal involves a two-way dialogue, but the distinction I wish to make is that this is about discussion on an individual's professional performance. In this section, I will focus on dialogue between manager and direct report, and anything else coming under the general heading of 'appraisal'. Appraisal is distinct from the employee giving feedback about the organisation itself, which is covered later in Chapter 7.

---

6   A language-learning app, if you didn't know, designed to encourage little-and-often learning.

The desire for extensive, and apparently 'instant', feedback has come as a surprise to many managers. A common attitude from the older generations was that time with your manager on a one-to-one basis was strictly limited. The less frequently it happened, the better. The thought of being 'called to your manager's office' was not an attractive one. Workplaces were more hierarchical with a more formal culture on average than we see today, so such a request usually meant bad news or an unwelcome increase in your workload. A bit like being sent to the headteacher's office.[7]

Appraisal, or 'performance management', systems have a bad name among many. Typical reasons include a lack of meaningful objectives, what will happen (or not) if those objectives are met, the quality of the dialogue, and how connected these metrics are to an employee's actual job. It is often said that appraisal should be a 'process rather than an event', but reality often looks different. From Gen Z's perspective, it absolutely has to be the former, and they need to be heavily involved.

The fact that Gen Z expects more feedback about their performance than previous generations does not surprise me. This expectation should not be misinterpreted as a longing for public recognition any more than for those from older generations. It is primarily about reassurance and guidance.

Seeking feedback comes from a desire to improve, and because doing good work and helping others are the right things to do. Among Gen X leaders, it often seems to be mistaken for narcissism,

---

7   From one perspective, this is stereotypical, and I am not claiming every single person had the same relationship with their manager. But it was also far less common for managers to have any form of training or ongoing professional development. How someone should manage or lead was a far less common topic than today.

and a wish for people to be told how fantastic they are over and over again. I imagine there are many employees from every age group who would be very happy to be endlessly reminded of their qualities, but for Gen Z this is not enough. Unless it is accompanied by detail on what comes next, then positive feedback alone is not particularly useful.

It is true that the world of social media has taught all its users that 'feedback' on posts can come thick and fast[8], including through the number of impressions granted by each algorithm with engagement in the form of likes and comments. There may be something in the idea that this level of responsiveness has had an impact on the workplace, but it would be wrong to make the assumption that young professionals cannot differentiate between the two.

Ultimately, Gen Z's approach to feedback at work is another example of their pragmatic approach, and it comes from a good place. There is also a return of the apprehension element here: if you are not getting feedback, there may be something wrong.

Ingraining detailed feedback at school

I am from a generation of teachers and school leaders who have done a lot to ingrain expectations around feedback into Gen Z. If you have not seen such a diagram before, or at least not in an educational context, this is a very basic example of a Question Level Analysis.

---

8   If you would like to hear a poignant description of this aspect of social media, listen to 'Numbers' by Weezer from their wonderful and underrated album 'OK Human'. Thirty minutes of listening bliss.

	Q1	Q2	Q3	Q4	Q5	Q6	Q7	Q8	Q9
Student 1		grey			grey	black	grey		grey
Student 2				grey			black	black	black
Student 3									black
Student 4	black	black			black	black	black	black	black
Student 5			black					grey	
Student 6		grey			grey		black	grey	grey
Student 7	black	black		grey		grey		grey	grey
Student 8									grey
Student 9					black				
Student 10				grey				black	

Figure 10: Example of a Question Level Analysis
from a mock (practice) examination

This is the kind of feedback Generation Z has been used to getting in their school career. It is generated from an assessment of some description, most often an internal examination in preparation for the real thing.

The diagram above is an excerpt from a spreadsheet that came into common use around in the early 2010s, as the eldest Gen Z were starting their secondary school years. The Qs represent questions on an examination paper, for any subject, and how well each student performed on each one. This one has three possibilities, based on a traffic light methodology but I have seen (and been responsible for) more.[9]

---

9   It is, trust me, possible to go over the top with this stuff. A 'traffic light' system is fine in principle, but having three colours tends to mean a lot can drift to the middle. The same applies to a customer survey where there are three possible answers. I have seen five-colour models and those continuous colour strips which slowly move from red to green.

In this example, a blank square means that the student performed very well on the question (the equivalent of a green traffic light), grey means average performance (orange) and black weak performance (red). From this, each student can have their own version which identifies priority areas for revision and practice. It is good feedback for teachers too, in that whatever the topic was for Q3 has clearly been taught well, but there is much to do for Q9. It offers a much higher level of precision than being told you got 62% in a test or a B on a paper.

In order for a student to become green in every question, resources are made available to them, the planning for the sequence of lessons adapted and so on. I have seen various examples of students having access to a document with hyperlinked videos and practice questions for every topic where their score was anything less than 100%. A Personalised Learning Checklist[10] can be formed from the information, providing a highly bespoke tool for revision purposes.

If you are reading this thinking you are used to this kind of granular dashboard approach in the workplace, but not at school, you'd be correct. The sense of your GCSEs or O levels, for example, as a strategically planned campaign picking off every last topic and spare mark with the school putting everything in your lap that you might ever need may not have been your experience. You might also think that students' outcomes would be different without any of this, and without high levels of teacher and school accountability alongside. You would be correct in this too.

It is not just the precision available here, but the quantity. A set of 10 questions can form fewer than a third of a single examination paper. For school students in England, they can easily have 20+ examinations overall[viii], across 8-20 courses, all taken in a single

---

10   I am not sure whether PiXL, and its founder Sir John Rowling, invented the phrase but I will give credit here anyway.

summer setting, and with up to three full sets of mock examinations in the year leading up to it. The entire picture for a GCSE-age student (14-16) could be several hundred questions or topics. It has not been conducive to the mental health of young people.

The precision of feedback is one reason why the quality of examination results has gone up. It is also why grade boundaries have moved up in response to students and their teachers getting ahead of the tactics. Governments tend to bristle at 'examinations are getting easier' headlines, and examination boards respond accordingly.[ix] The shift from the A* to G to 9 to 1 grading system was another attempt at a solution.

In summary, Gen Z is not just used to knowing how well they have performed, but also a dialogue around their performance that runs something like:

- Here are the question areas and topics where you need to improve.
- This is by how much you need to improve in order to achieve your target.
- Here are sets of equivalent questions to practise with.
- Extra lessons have been put on for you at this time.
- Here are links to YouTube videos, or equivalent, that show you how to do it step by step.
- This is the electronic resource you can use to get automated feedback on the progress you have made.
- While you are here, this student performed well on a question where you did not. Go and talk to them and find out how they did it.

This is not just about feedback, it is also about:
- A high level of precision so that the fastest possible rate of progress can be made.
- A swift turnaround so you can make a start (just one way in which expectations on teachers and workload in general have grown).

- Providing all necessary resources in one place without a student having to spend time looking.

There are two key inherent weaknesses within this whole system. The first is perhaps the most relevant to those who recruit and retain young staff. Accountability for student outcomes has moved increasingly towards the teachers over time. The level of 'service' students receive to enable them to smash their examinations is unparalleled compared to the start of my career. Naturally, this is a positive development in terms of exam results. The disadvantage is that students have not had to work out for themselves how to do well to the same extent as in the past, because resources are put in their hands. This done-for-you feedback is unlikely to prepare students for the world of work and the expectations of their managers from older generations.

This cuts both ways, of course. Throughout this book, I argue that older managers need to adapt to their young staff more than they often anticipate. Modern methods of improving examination results have meant employers have work to do to ensure their employees are independent. Young professionals need a higher level of engagement from their managers both to point out the resources which exist and coach them through other aspects of their development.

Secondly, despite the fact that students have done better over time, the pressures of England's examination system have had other side effects. This includes those who might achieve the examination results they wanted, but at a cost to their mental health. It also includes the numbers not in education, employment or training mentioned in Chapter 4 and those of school age not on a school roll at all. [11]

---

11   This is now over 100,000. For clarity, I am not talking about those who have a school to go to and don't attend, but those of school age who are not even on a school roll. I am not against home education but am deeply suspicious of why the numbers have grown so quickly in such a short time. This started before the pandemic.

This has implications for organisations and their recruitment, including young adults having fantastic academic records but suffering from poor mental health that affects productivity, as covered earlier. It also includes those who missed out on a lot of the school experience and are now entering employment.

Strategies to provide precise feedback and a path to improvement

The frequency and precision of the feedback received at school is one reason why it is not enough these days for an organisation, or a manager, just to say what went well or badly. Broad, hazy feedback is not enough, in the same way that broad, hazy appraisal objectives were never enough.

The workplace does not need to replicate the school practice I just described, not least because it may be inappropriate, unhelpful or inefficient. Doing so could encourage 'learned helplessness', which is hard to shift and generally counterproductive.

Even if it should not replicate the detail of school, feedback must still be frequent and precise, as well as accompanied by easily accessible resources that help the employee improve. The average Gen Zer is able to handle a more detailed level of feedback and advice than many of their older managers imagine. They may well be more resilient to some of the more difficult areas too, if the road to improvement is clearly signposted.

If, for example, a Gen X manager does not want to provide the feedback and resources because they did not have them or because it will enable employees to pass through the ranks quicker than they were able to, then the issue is with the manager. If the outcome is that individuals are promoted earlier in their career than the older generations believe they 'should have been', then it is time to look at the training programmes and job descriptions, not the resourceful Gen Zer who has found their way through.

Feedback loops

All of this means there is a need for clarity and ground rules. Organisations need to be transparent about the methods for giving and receiving feedback that they have in place, and how they will operate. They also need to be clear about how much responsibility individual employees have to improve their own performance and the extent to which they will (and will not) signpost them. Where resources do not exist, or are fewer in number, organisations can at least be clear about the standards they expect about higher order skills such as problem-solving or strategic thinking.

Line management arrangements need some ground rules and clarity. If relevant information about performance is available to both manager and direct report without having to meet, this can save a lot of trouble. 'Holding on' to data that could easily be shared at any time also requires some justification these days, if it is not to be seen as a futile power battle.

These ground rules should include something about how available a manager can be for an employee. One who needs a lot of reassurance, for whatever reason, may need some lines drawn about how quickly an email response will come[12] or how often they should knock on the door.

---

12   This applies in both directions. It may generate some anxiety for an employee to feel cut off, even for a few hours, but ultimately an organisation will need them to work it out for themselves or from their colleagues.

That availability also applies to line management meetings. My coaching work tells me how common it can be, across a range of professions, to have a poor experience. This can include:

- Line management meetings cancelled at short notice and with no reason.
- Little or no preparation for the meeting by the manager.
- So-called one-to-ones becoming a one-way communication lacking genuine dialogue and listening.
- Line management meetings becoming the only venue for communication with no replies to emails or phone calls in between.

Ultimately, an organisation will need to set an expectation about frequency and duration of such meetings. Better still, they should consult along the way. If the pattern is not adhered to by managers, they will find more communication coming their way seeking more and more feedback than they prefer to give or have time for. They may also find it has a more detrimental effect on well-being than they anticipate.

Synchronous communication

Managers of Gen Z may be surprised by these figures from the Society of Human Resource Management.[x] They are originally pre-pandemic (2018), but nothing I have heard or read since indicates significant change in the trend. In response to the question 'how do Gen Zs prefer to be communicated with?', synchronous forms of communication (face to face 43% and phone 14%) were more popular than asynchronous forms (text 24%, email 11% and social media 8%). It is a sign of the times that 'virtual calls' was not given as an option, but again they are a synchronous form of communication. Note that this underestimates the true picture, as non-synchronous modes of communication, text, email and social media, can also be used synchronously.[13]

Non-synchronous communication may be more easily accessed and ubiquitous, but that does not mean it is preferable nor effective. Key forms of synchronous communication such as the Zoom call or an in-person conversation also offer a much greater level of information, such as tone of voice and body language. They enable participants to ascertain whether the other party is truly listening and showing empathy or understanding. All of this helps generate a sense of authenticity and, most importantly, trust.

Synchronous communication offers Gen Zers the opportunity to develop the soft skills they know they need. If you want them to learn from you, and vice versa, then get in the room with them.

While the above survey was completed before virtual meetings became the go-to option during the pandemic, the popularity of FaceTime amongst Gen Z was long established before Covid hit. A video meeting may not be quite the same as one in 3D, not least because eye contact is technically impossible. Participants can either look at their camera or the screen, but not both, unlike in a face-to-face meeting. It is still more raw, requires those involved to think on their feet, and consider their position on the basis of what they hear.

Gen Z is absolutely not immune to taking feedback and acting upon it. They may demand more of it, and more often, than you feel is reasonable, but this is not coming from a place of impatience. The challenge for organisations is to ensure feedback is sufficiently

---

13   As one example, the WhatsApp conversation where two or more parties are fully engaged in their responses, responsive enough for it to feel like a conversation and not engaged in any other activity. Let's not go there with those endless 'reply all' email chains.

frequent and precise, and that the resources are easily accessible to facilitate improvement.

The Myth of Instant falls apart when the details are in place. If your biggest issue is that your young staff are blasting their way through every opportunity and consistently keen to improve at pace, then you do not have a problem at all.

Endnotes

i   Oldham, M., Holmes, J., Whitaker, V., Fairbrother, H., & Curtis, P. (n.d.). *Youth drinking in decline.* https://www.sheffield.ac.uk/news/polopoly_fs/1.806889!/file/Oldham_Holmes_Youth_drinking_in_decline_FINAL.pdf

ii Demography Team. (2024, June 19). *Marriages in England and Wales – Office for National Statistics.* https://www.ons.gov.uk/peoplepopulationandcommunity/birthsdeathsandmarriages/marriagecohabitationandcivilpartnerships/bulletins/marriagesinenglandandwalesprovisional/2021and2022

iii Walker, P. R. a. A. (2024, October 28). *Fertility rate in England and Wales drops to new low.* BBC News. https://www.bbc.co.uk/news/articles/cnvj3j27nmro

iv Demography Team (2024b, October 22). *National life tables – life expectancy in England and Wales – Office for National Statistics.* https://www.ons.gov.uk/peoplepopulationandcommunity/birthsdeathsandmarriages/lifeexpectancies/bulletins/nationallifetablesunitedkingdom/2021to2023

v   Hopkirk, N. (2023, June 8) *What's the average first-time buyer deposit by region in 2023?* https://www.zoopla.co.uk/discover/property-news/whats-the-average-first-time-buyer-deposit-by-region/

vi FreshGround. (2024b, June 5). *Why is a takeaway coffee so expensive? FreshGround.* https://freshground.co.uk/learning-hub/why-is-a-takeaway-coffee-so-expensive/#:~:text=It%E2%80%99s%20a%20booming%20business%20with,why%20the%20high%20price%20tag

vii *UK average rent inflation over time – Property Beacon.* (2023, September 17). Property Beacon. https://www.propertybeacon.co.uk/uk-average-rent-inflation/

viii Think Student. (2023, August 20). *How many GCSE exams do students have to take? (By subject).* https://thinkstudent.co.uk/how-many-gcse-exams-do-students-have-to-take/

ix Ofqual. (2016). *An investigation into the 'Sawtooth Effect' in GCSE and AS / A level assessments.* https://assets.publishing.service.gov.uk/media/5a814f3c40f0b623026969bb/an-investigation-into-the-sawtooth-effect-in-gcse-as-and-a-level-assessments.pdf

x   Miller, J. (2023, December 21). A 16-Year-Old explains 10 things you need to know about Generation Z. *SHRM*. https://www.shrm.org/topics-tools/news/hr-magazine/16-year-old-explains-10-things-need-to-know-generation-z#:~:text=Gen%20Z%20Is%20Connected&text=While%20it's%20often%20assumed%20that,-ways%20to%20be%20fully%20satisfied.

6

The Myth of Apathy

Before the internet, before social media and before inboxes were lovingly stuffed with hundreds of unread messages every time you walked away from your desk for two hours, life was simpler. Life was also relatively linear, with a tried-and-tested 'birth, school, work, death'[i] model. Some of those who went to school also went to university. The really adventurous[1] either had a year out beforehand or took a master's degree afterwards. If you got a 'proper' job, there was a fair chance that it could be in the same organisation for the rest of your working life, should you choose, or at least you would remain in the industry.

There was a reasonable possibility that the workplace would form the basis for much of your life beyond work, particularly if you had

---

1   And often very well resourced too. I am not pretending that anyone other than a small, privileged percentage was in this category. I did not do the former, but did the latter, spending the money my granddad left in his will on the tuition fees for my masters. My memory of the early '90s is that the year out was the more popular option, should the opportunity arise.

moved away from home to take the job. Lifelong friends would be made from post-work socialising, particularly on Fridays. It was a place to find your significant other and share your weekend exploits all in the same physical place. With the rarest of exceptions[2], you had met in person all those you knew.

The relative linearity of life meant that a lot could rest on the workplace, in a way that presents more as a risky single point of failure in this day and age. Your current income, future career prospects, flatmates, partner and social life could all depend on it. Consequently, the level to which employees were invested in work could be far more significant than today. I am not saying that no one moved on, changed their industry or that everyone relied wholly on work for their social scene. However, searching for a new job was a far more laborious process, and without dating sites and apps, the workplace was relied upon for relationships to a degree. People may have stuck with a job they were lucky to have, because when an industry went under and jobs were gone, they were gone, as happened in the coal mines near where I grew up.

Technology has broadened the range of choices for many, not only about where individuals work but how they work. A physical workplace for five days per week with 20 or so days of paid leave per year is increasingly the rarity rather than the norm.

Gen Z has come into the workplace not only with more choice about how they live the professional phases of their lives, but also how they spent their time in their formative years. This has affected their approach to the workplace.

---

2   By which, I basically mean pen pals. Despite the popularity of the phrase, I'm not sure how much of a thing this really was, beyond a couple of excruciatingly written postcards exchanged with a student at a partner school. Pen yes, pal no.

Workplace observations

Here are some examples of what my Gen X peers and the media have said about Gen Z.

- "Quiet quitting describes it very well. In most cases, it does not start from a high base. They turn up, do not commit and then slide off to something else. You can see it coming."
- "They have no commitment to the organisation at all, despite what we have invested in them. They turn up, do their two years, get qualified then they are off. It is all very transactional. Some of them do not even pretend any more."
- "If there is anything that presents as a slightly better opportunity elsewhere, they are off. Sometimes they find out the hard way that the grass is not greener, and their new company discovers they were a stepping stone as well."
- "Work social events are quite sad these days. When I started, we all went to the pub as a staff after work on Friday. It was really important bonding time and we had a lot of fun. People would let their hair down. Now there are not many people there at all, just those who have worked for the company for some years."
- "They do not understand the value of being in the office. It is about camaraderie and a sense of working together. But they just want to work from home, or somewhere other than work. Work is about more than a bunch of tasks."
- "When we do have a work call, I want to see them. I want to know they are engaging. Apparently asking for cameras to be on is crossing the line these days. Speaking into the ether is not a pleasant experience."
- "Anything that involves a team approach can be a real struggle. They just want to work on their own, or with someone their own age."
- "You can forget anything that is 'above and beyond'. It is pretty

much working to rule from the start. They do not recognise the value of others who do so either, even if their achievements lead to collective success for them."

- "There is often very little interest in what is happening in the rest of the industry. It is as though they restrict their engagement as far as possible because they may not be around for long, either with us or the industry. Knowing about industry trends or developments seems to be someone else's job."

- "As soon as they have done the same task a few times, they expect to be moved on to something else. Of course we understand the value of efficiency, and would do it another way if we could, but it does not apply to everything. Some aspects of work are repetitive and stay that way."

A generation shaped by austerity

Exploring the Myth of Apathy begins with some questions. What is there for Gen Z to invest in? How can they get involved and why should they choose to engage? What is in it for them if they do?

Primarily, I am referring to financial prudence in this section. The clearest starting point for this can be seen in the graph below. In particular, I argue that two dramatic global events affected Gen Z at least as much as anyone else. These were the GFC in 2008 and the Covid-19 pandemic that transformed our lives in 2020.

The GFC was the most severe worldwide economic crisis since the Great Depression of the 1930s. A government bailout of many millions of pounds, dollars[3] and other currencies prevented the entire

---

3   For those of you who were not around to witness it, or for some reason would like to revisit it, I strongly recommend the film *The Big Short*. It does not shy away from explaining the economics, and the way it does so only adds to the drama.

banking system going under. Although the most catastrophic failure was avoided, the impact was highly significant nonetheless.

In retrospect, we did not realise how good we had it in the years leading up to the crash. Although the period of time between the recovery from the GFC and the pandemic seem to follow a similar pattern to what came before, there are two factors to consider.

Primarily, there was much lower growth on average in the years following the crash. The economic losses incurred also took some time to wipe out. The years after the GFC were far less prosperous for the older Gen Z than those experienced by the older Millennials as they entered the workplace in the early 2000s. Then the economic impact of the pandemic may have been extremely severe, but it also followed a difficult period.

The second reason[4] is related to the first. What became known as the austerity programme featured repeated and extensive cuts to education, welfare and local government. In the UK, VAT was raised to what felt like an eye-watering 20% at the time and has stayed there ever since.

When the GFC was happening, the oldest Gen Zs were in their first month of secondary school and the youngest were some years away from being born. The banks that went under took many businesses, jobs and homes with them. The youngest generation is always going to be affected more by public spending cuts than the rest of the population, as they depend upon those services more.

---

4   There is no universal agreement from both ends of the political spectrum in the UK. Without getting into the debate, I doubt David Cameron and George Osborne anticipated that rates of growth would stay so low for so long. I imagine they would still dispute the use of the word 'austerity' as well, but it fell into common usage so I am sticking with it.

Austerity meant fewer resources for schools and devastating cuts to youth services. Economic uncertainty also led to hiring freezes and, therefore, fewer job opportunities for young professionals.

The 2010s demonstrated that neither gains made in previous generations could be guaranteed, nor lessons would be learned from economic disasters. It may be a cliche that a key lesson of history is that its lessons are not learned, but the evidence supports it.

Despite the crash, business investment in the UK continued on an upward trend for years afterwards. That plateaued from 2016 onwards (the same year as the Brexit vote), then nose-dived in the pandemic. Optimism in the UK has not been high for a sustained period of time. Check the graph from the Office of National Statistics[5] below.

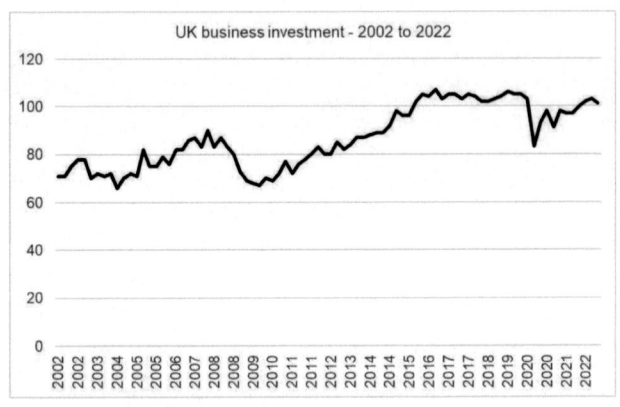

Figure 11: Business investment in the UK from 2002 to 2022[ii]

Quiet quitting

This brings me to 'quiet quitting'. The phrase was popularised by a TikTok video by Zaid Khan in July 2022. It means that employees

---

5   Index is referenced against Quarter 1 2022 which equals 100.

reach the point where they do the absolute minimum of what they need to do in order to hang on to their job. Over an extended period, they stick rigidly to their job description, restrict their contributions in meetings and may have higher-than-average levels of absenteeism.

I am sometimes asked what the difference is between quiet quitting and working to rule.[6] The answer is that they are similar, but quiet quitting represents a continuous decline rather than a mode of operation that could be switched on and off. It may also ride a fine line between an organisation handling the issue informally or via formal procedures.

The speed at which the phrase came into common usage indicates that it struck a nerve, both with Gen Z and their employers. I am not going to claim that quiet quitting is not a thing, but I do suggest it does not apply to the whole generation. Gen Z will invest, but there are good reasons why it may not come naturally to all of them, and it has much to do with confidence.

Economic confidence

Gen Z has good reason to be less confident about future economic prosperity, even beyond the cost of living crisis and pandemic recovery, both of which can be described as 'ongoing' at the time of writing. Deloitte's 2024 Gen Z and Millennials' global survey[iii] showed that less than a third of both believed the economic situation in their country would improve in the next year.

The pandemic may have led to a more pessimistic outlook on the economy, but the numbers were not strong even before Covid-19.

---

6   Typically, working to rule has been a minor form of industrial action, undertaken when goodwill between managers and staff has broken down and none is then offered by staff. They work their contracted hours and no more.

On average, Millennials are slightly more pessimistic than Gen Z, but by definition they are also older. The fact that Gen Z is coming out of their school education similarly despondent about the future feels particularly depressing. Pessimism at such a young age is not a good place to be.

Gen Z also suffered economically from the pandemic in economic terms, arguably more than any other generation. A survey of U.S. adults from Vox in 2020 showed that it was the younger generation who was more likely to lose their job or take a cut in pay[iv]. As with the GFC, every generation was affected. As ever, the variations within generations will be greater than those between, and not just on the basis of age either.

In terms of shaping the outlook of a generation, the key point is this: by the time the oldest Gen Zs got to their early twenties, there had been a key economic disaster that shaped their teenage years, the Brexit referendum, which had significant implications for their future and in which few were old enough to participate, then a further economic disaster as soon as they got to the workplace.

Those on the lowest incomes were also hit hardest by the pandemic. This included those who used the gig economy for part or all of their income, and those who experienced the misfortune of being 'last in, first out'. Any impact on the lowest incomes is going to affect the youngest disproportionately given earnings are lower at the start of your working life.

All of this has led to Gen Z being a generation much more disposed to save, as far-fetched as that possibility appears to be right now. My analysis of this is that it does not necessarily represent saving for a more prosperous future, rather mitigating against the next disaster.

A key task for Gen X in early professional life was to save for a deposit for a house or a flat. Renting was sufficiently affordable so saving could happen to a greater or lesser extent. Many then went on to exploit[7] this security to buy further properties with the introduction of buy-to-let mortgages in the mid-1990s. Rent was commonly described as 'dead money'. Although this was and is true, at the time it inferred that anyone renting in the long term needed to get their act together. Paying the bills did not represent an achievement in the same way as it does for so many today.

Others got on the housing ladder and moved their way up. Those with a mortgage in place before the GFC then discovered a key benefit if they survived it. Interest rates fell to record low levels and stayed there for well over a decade. The experience of ownership became cheaper than anticipated. The fixed rate period of a mortgage would end and payments fell, often substantially.

As property prices increased, the ability to save diminished for those who had not got as far as purchasing, because rent absorbed a higher proportion of income. Young Millennial professionals either moved back in with their families to save, or moved somewhere cheaper. Even then this proved beyond many whose 'temporary' circumstances became a lot more permanent.

Gen Z has been faced with the terrible position of an economy with sclerotic levels of growth accompanied by a significant increase

---

7   Controversial choice of word? Possibly. Easy for me to say as well, given that my career in schools meant a more-than-solid pension as my peers saw their own prospects of having one disappear, and commercial alternatives were not as attractive. Buying a second property became the equivalent of a pension to many. I would draw a distinction between that and developing a property portfolio, seeking every possible chance to raise the rent.

in rent, as only one feature of the cost of living crisis. They live in smaller spaces and with more people in them. On top of that, the Covid lockdowns meant working from home in a space not ideal for the task. The organisations they worked for found they could make savings in renting smaller spaces. Graduates got their job, then found no designated space to work beyond the room they slept in.

Declining faith in institutions

All of this presents an issue for organisations, and perhaps larger corporations in particular. Generation Z does not have as much faith in them. The same is true for governments, political parties and other institutions.

Gen Z not only sees a future in working around institutions, but also does so out of necessity, rather than a sense of idealism. From their perspective, traditional ways of doing things have not worked. Given this, it does not matter if the old ones are disrupted. Furthermore, 'disrupting the system' is not necessarily part of the journey to building a new one either. This would only lead to a new set of institutions. It is not just the current institutions that are problematic, but the concept of institutions per se.

'Institutions' tend to be controlled by older generations. They have multi-layered organisation charts to battle through over the sustained period of a career. Those who run them do not have a vested interest in changing the status quo. The same applies to not tackling key issues of climate change, representation in the workplace at senior level, and the growing gap between rich and poor.

Consequently, many employees are on a back foot to begin with, particularly those working in well-established organisations. Unless this is understood, it is difficult to make progress. This presents serious issues for leaders seeking to recruit and retain the best of Gen Z.

Placing importance on values

Even in advance of the pandemic, there was good evidence that Gen Z was extremely interested in achieving value for money. The phrase 'cost of living crisis' may have come into common usage as the pandemic subsided, the war in Ukraine began, Liz Truss' disastrous seven weeks as Prime Minister ran their course and the rate of inflation rocketed more than 20 times[8] over, but there were plenty from Gen Z who felt it beforehand.

The concept of value does not just refer to price. Food is a key interest for Gen Z, but it comes with an expectation of being very locally sourced and not racking up food miles at any cost just to get the ingredient. Such ethical issues really matter. Increasingly, the same applies to other aspects of consumerism, particularly clothes. The success of Depop and Vinted does not just represent Gen Z's love of vintage clothing, but also their eye for a side hustle and an understanding of environmental impact.

The before-mentioned Deloitte survey identifies that Gen Z 'chooses financial stability against enjoyment by two to one', and to a much greater extent than Millennials.

Significantly, and perhaps conversely, they also value salary less than any previous generation. This needs a little explanation. I am not saying they do not want to get paid, or have the best chance of meeting the eye-watering cost of living, but there is also a limit to the extent they will trade their values to climb the ladder. They need to see the same applies for those who lead and manage them.

---

8   Just in case you blinked at that statistic, here are the facts. Inflation was 0.5% in September 2020 and 11.1% in October 2022.

The economic and global circumstances inherited by Gen Z have shifted their outlook compared to previous generations and ensured that prudence is a key characteristic. Financial stability may have been desired by every generation, but it has become harder to obtain for the youngest adults, and far more fragile once there. Assuming that a heftier pay packet is the sole solution to this problem will not aid any organisation seeking to recruit and retain the best.

Understanding and responding appropriately to this dilemma is fundamental for organisations in meeting the key challenges posed by Gen Z.

As I touched on in Chapter 2, Gen Z is not the only generation to enter their young professional lives in times of economic adversity. My year of birth puts me in the middle of Gen X. The recession of the early 1990s coincided with my graduation. Many employers steered clear of the graduate careers fairs[9] as they did not need the young recruits. The younger Baby Boomers had the recession of the mid-1970s with the spike in oil prices and the three-day week. The older Boomers were young enough to remember rationing, which did not end until 1954, a full nine years after VE day.

Gen Z has not seen an enforced three-day week, rationing or mass unemployment. What is different about Gen Z's circumstances is a lack of expectation that their economic circumstances will improve. Older generations are those who own the property. New property that is built tends to disappear to those who already own one or more. When it comes to climate change, a so-called 'ambition' to limit the global average temperature rise to 1.5 degrees[10] is neither ambitious enough nor are serious efforts being made to make even

---

9   Or, as they were rather quaintly collectively called, the Milkround.

10   Already passed across the 12-month period from February 2023 to January 2024 in the wake of El Nino.

that a reality. Their generational disadvantages are structural and locked in.

Strategies to enhance collaboration opportunities

Is all this talk of disengagement making you feel apathetic too? Here's the antidote. Do as Gen Z do and seek to connect and engage.

Collaboration comes more naturally to Gen Z than any previous generation. Their upbringing as digital natives has meant that working together is second nature. They are the first generation where kids could play on their games consoles together but in different locations. Their social media groups and online communities have been built, ground rules established, moderated, discarded and rebuilt. The preference for a 'collab' is well-rooted from their life experience.

The same applies to sharing where they are online, along with what they are doing and who they are with. I am not saying that everyone in Gen Z shares their life online with those they know or in public for anyone to find. In fact, there's a good case for saying that they do so less on average than Millennials, but they have only known a time when it was both possible and normalised. Gen Z grew up with the concept of the social media influencer who did not rely on long-established forms of media such as newspapers, film or television to build a mass audience.

All of this is very positive given that some of the issues raised above, like quiet quitting, are not conducive to ensuring multi-generational workplaces are harmonious. Again, as with every other myth, I am not saying that the entire generation is immediately seeking collaborative opportunities. I am saying that they have more experience of collaboration than those who came before them. They are likely to find it odd when any workplace that does not value it as a way of improving both efficacy and efficiency. They may also find it more comfortable to collaborate using methods where older generations lack familiarity and confidence.

The extensive experience that Gen Z has had in collaborative work has led them to an expectation that it will be a core feature of their working life. Why would an employer not want their employees to operate in this way? Surely, the same applies to their co-workers too?

In the avoidance of generational stereotyping to make a point, I will say this instead: productive workplaces require employees to learn from each other's experiences, perspectives and ideas, including across generations.

In the UK, the percentage of those aged 65 or older doubled in two decades.[11] As retirement ages climb ever higher, along with the numbers who never bought property and will always be paying rent[12], this is only going to continue to rise.

Ultimately, cross-generational collaboration is the only way to go, whether in the form of the project team, working party, task force or away day. The cross-generational team enables fresh ideas, synergies from skills and experience and the satisfaction from collective effort.

These are some examples of how a collaborative and coherent multi-generational workplace can become reality. Given the focus of this book, I do not want to spend too much time on the older generations. The examples below operate on the basis that, if they are good for the workplace, they will be good for Gen Z and vice versa.

---

11   4.6% in 2001 to 11.2% in 2022.

12   There is a common perception that the Covid-19 pandemic drove the significant increase in those of retirement age returning to work. In reality, this trend started many years in advance.

1. Wear your values and expectations on your sleeve

Organisations need to determine what they want to be the same for everyone. This ensures a strong foundation for collaboration because the ground rules have been set. It sounds almost too simple. Yet as workplaces become increasingly diverse, organisations can shy away from answering a key question. What must everyone working here have in common?

Although the more diverse the workplace, the harder it might be to achieve alignment, that is even more of a reason to make it happen. It is not enough to say that, because people are so different, they cannot be on the same page these days. Diversity makes it even more important to bring people together.

This means clarity about key areas such as core values, shared goals and non-negotiables, and involvement in putting them together. The trick is to ensure that the list is small enough so staff can refer to it, but even more so that they can live and breathe it.

If mutual respect or an inclusive ethos, for example, is a core feature of life in your organisation, think about these questions. What should that look like in practice? Who is expected to uphold it? How will you know what employees make of how it is going? How do you know whether employees have divergent definitions of what this means, rather than just one?

This conversation needs to be opened up across the workforce, with time and resources dedicated to ensure full participation. If you want staff to be committed to it, they need to be involved in forming it. Your Gen Z staff will be at least as committed to this as anyone else.

An increasingly diverse workplace, including on the basis of age, demands that time and attention is paid to ensuring that not only are expectations and values clear, but also upheld. Selecting some words for effect is a particularly bad look.

2. Mentoring works both ways

Reverse mentoring programmes can add considerable value, particularly when time is allocated to them. There is a traditional view that Gen Z can teach older colleagues about new technologies and digital trends, whereas older generations can share industry knowledge and professional experience.

Both of these carry value. It is much better to approach this from the perspective that both groups can learn from each other's perspectives and strengths, irrespective of years of experience. It does not always need a formal agenda to start with, but getting this right means that older generations need to be receptive to new thinking.

Perspectives on equity, diversity and inclusion might vary across generations as a whole, although this is also a good example of where perspectives are likely to vary more within them. Individual stories of how an individual's outlook came to be formed, with occasional paradigm shifts along the way, can be very powerful.

Organisations that enable professional (and personal) development opportunities with groups of diverse colleagues open up a lot of positive possibilities. A workforce that collaborates in order to learn from each other develops the potential to solve a lot of problems. Putting Gen Z at the heart of this gives them the opportunity to show what they can do best.

3. Communication boundaries

Everyone has a responsibility to understand and to be understood, and collaboration requires open dialogue across generations. An issue of the modern age is the dazzling range of options for communication, and implications for how they can be used in practice.

Whichever generation you belong to, if a workplace has Slack channels, emails, WhatsApp groups, Teams chat, shared drives and social media accounts all operating 24/7 and without restriction, you will not have effective communication. It is very easy to end up with a lot being said, but without much of it having an impact (should anyone even be able to find it).

It is also easy for an individual to be missed out of the loop from the new group they were not added to, if notifications are not set up or if yet another message disappears into the unread pile. Communication should be judged by how and whether a message was received, rather than how well the sender thought it was constructed on their preferred platform.

For a lot of Gen Z, X (formerly Twitter) is where middle-aged folks go to shout at each other. For a lot of Gen X, a Facebook account, using WhatsApp for messages and possibly one other platform is more than enough. In the workplace, there is a need for some common ground.

Accessing a new platform does not come naturally to everyone, so training will be required along with some follow-up and a simple set of ground rules. Gen Z is very used to processing large numbers of messages in a very short period of time, and managing the challenge of the ever-buzzing phone, but that does not necessarily hold for everyone else.

The same might apply to using the phone for telephone calls.[v] Increasingly, I am told by clients that this is an issue, specifically a lack of willingness to pick up the phone by some young staff. We now spend far less time talking live on telephone calls, now down to an average of 5.5 minutes per day[vi] (albeit with wide variations[vii]).[13] If it is essential for the workplace, then training needs to be available in the same way as for any other form of technology, as do common expectations with a rationale.

Ground rules may also be necessary around the formality of language or the use of acronyms to ensure accessibility. Furthermore an organisation may need to decide whether particular forms of communication should be face-to-face, digital or written.

4. Employee engagement matters

If the annual questionnaire (or worse still, a mere survey) is your sole form of employee engagement, it is time for a rethink. **Engagement needs to be a collaborative activity that allows for dialogue across a multi-generational workforce as well as between management and employees.**

The short 'pulse' survey to capture feedback on a particular topic is a valuable tool, and allows for little-and-often engagement. Even better to ask people to complete it live in a town hall-type meeting where the outcomes can be seen instantly, with a breakout opportunity to discuss the findings and determine what the organisation can do next. Working parties, social events, the staff kitchen and professional

---

13   I have found it hard to quantify the extent to which this has fallen, but as general context I remember telephone boxes having queues as standard. The later reference indicates by a third on average since 1999, although that feels quite low against the issue as described to me.

development activities are all opportunities for both employee engagement and collaboration across staff. While working together on a large project carries value, the same is also true of the smaller ongoing options.

Networking events are generally thought of as external, where employees of one organisation meet another, as opposed to internal where employees from the same organisation get to know each other better. These informal gatherings can be used to foster connections across age groups in person, allow the older generations to meet the emerging talent, and help Gen Z to expand their professional network. They can also provide a valuable support network, particularly for workplaces which are primarily remote.

In stepping away from the Myth of Apathy, the key is ensuring that engagement activities and collaboration opportunities are an ongoing process rather than a one-time event. Seeking engagement in such a way will provide the best demonstration of why the concept that Gen Z is uninvested is a myth. They are not invested in the same ways as older generations were. However, when strategies are implemented in the right way and with a clarity of purpose, Gen Z can and will model the value of collaboration for everyone else.

Endnotes

i   Francis-Devine, B., Zaidi K. & Murray A. *Women and the UK Economy*. House of Commons. https://researchbriefings.files.parliament.uk/documents/SN06838/SN06838.pdf

ii Gross Capital Formation Team (2024, December 23). *Business investment in the UK – Office for National Statistics*. https://www.ons.gov.uk/economy/grossdomesticproductgdp/bulletins/businessinvestment/julytoseptember2024revisedresults

iii Deloitte. (2024). *2024 Gen Z and Millennial Survey*. https://www.deloitte.com/content/dam/assets-shared/docs/campaigns/2024/deloitte-2024-genz-millennial-survey.pdf?dlva=1

iv Collins, S. (2020, May 5). Why the Covid-19 economy is particularly devastating to millennials, in 14 charts. *Vox*. https://www.vox.com/2020/5/5/21222759/covid-19-recession-millennials-coronavirus-economic-impact-charts

v   Rufo, Y. (2024, August 26). *Why Gen Z & Millennials are hung up on answering the phone*. BBC News. https://www.bbc.co.uk/news/articles/crgklk3p70yo

vi *Call me maybe (not): a quarter of young people never answer the phone – Uswitch*. (n.d.). Uswitch. https://www.uswitch.com/media-centre/2024/04/Call-me-maybe-quarter-young-people-never-answer-phone/

vii Shermadovs. (2024, November 20). *The chart below shows the total number of minutes (in billions) of telephone calls in the UK, divided into three categories, from 1995-2002. Summarise the information by selecting and reporting the main features, and make comparisons where relevant.* Writing9. https://writing9.com/text/673d95f70b20930011f8116c-the-chart-below-shows-the-total-number-of-minutes-in-billions-of-telephone-calls-in-the-uk-divided-i

7

The Myth of Slack

When did the workplace get so casual? This is something workplace leaders complain about all the time. From a loose concept of deadlines to emojis in emails, what are Gen Z thinking? While these complaints may seem like Gen Z laziness (which we have already busted in the Myth of Lazy), I am defining slack a little differently here.

Laziness is different in two ways. First in terms of intention, laziness implies deliberate avoidance of work, as I set out in Chapter 3. Slack, on the other hand, infers a relaxed approach to getting things done. Second in terms of productivity, laziness implies low productivity, whereas slack is about reduced intensity, seeking shortcuts or starting later than the boss would prefer.

So, are Gen Z slack or just smart?

Workplace observations

Take a look at these attitudes from my peers and the media.

- "When I said they could work from home, that meant sticking to company hours. I called them and there was no reply for two hours. When they called me back much later, they said they had been to the gym. They do not seem to get that there is a difference between flexibility in where they work and how they work. Both need to be agreed. It is a weekday not the weekend."

- "They want to treat our policies as guidelines. If they think it is out of date or unnecessary, it is seen as voluntary. There is little sense of contractual obligations. They want to be persuaded to do something that has already been agreed."

- "Work-life balance tends to mean that work has to fit around their life, that they cannot stay beyond their official finish time no matter what is going on. The same can apply to the time they turn up. It would be great for everyone if their personal lives always came first, but that's not realistic."

- "There can be a reluctance to want to do anything in depth. The preference is always for the podcast and not the book. Some skills take a long time to learn and cannot be mastered from a two-hour online course, let alone a short video. Then they expect to be promoted quickly despite resisting learning anything in depth."

- "The way they address managers is horrific. They expect to be treated as equals, even if they have only just arrived, and when they aren't in return, they take offence."

- "It is embarrassing for me as a manager when members of my team miss deadlines. Yet when it happens, I am told that they should have had a few reminders. This is work, not a marketing campaign."

- "I get complaints that the work should have been broken down into more manageable parts. They got the job and need to work it out themselves. I'm not into spoon-feeding. I need them to stand on their own two feet."

- "Their language and tone in emails and online chats is all over the place, including with senior managers. They are so informal and do not understand why it is unprofessional. It is always 'Hi' rather than 'Dear', with emojis and acronyms not understood by those on the other end. Then there's the spelling. They do not get why this matters."

- "Some of them do not dress appropriately for work and strongly resist being told otherwise. They tell me that it should not matter how they dress because they do their work well. Their wardrobe is their wardrobe. That is what I hear. If we want them to dress differently, they say they should receive an allowance."

- "They expect to be able to walk into my office and start a conversation with me at any time. I am told that I should have an open-door policy, and the same applies to everyone else who is senior. My time is precious. They need to respect that more."

A diligent generation

In short, Gen X managers are frustrated with a casual attitude to conduct, quality and appearance. But is Gen Z really so slack? While I hear the frustrations, and will deal with them in this chapter, I argue that diligence is a key characteristic of Generation Z.

University degree classifications are a good place to start. The table below summarises the degree classifications from English universities across the 2010s, as produced by the independent regulator. Although these particular figures only cover English universities, the pattern is similar across the UK.

	2010-11	2018-19
First	16%	29%
Upper second	52%	50%
Other	33%	21%

Figure 12: Degree classifications in English universities across the 2010s

The figures show a significant rise in the average degree classification over this period. In the mid-1990s, when it was still Generation X that was graduating, the combined figure for first and upper second (2:1) alone was less than 50%[ii]. In the mid-2000s, as Millennials completed their degrees, the combined figure moved up to the mid-50s. It is now over three quarters.

Note that figures for 2020 and 2021 are not comparable with this period, as they were the two years affected by the pandemic. As was the case with secondary schools, universities had to find a new way of awarding qualifications. This led to a further increase in outcomes, including the percentage of first-class degrees rising to almost 40%. Since 2023, outcomes started to move back to pre-pandemic levels, in common with schools.

Approximately two-thirds of 'other' is represented by lower seconds (2:2), and the rest is evenly split between a third class degree and not passing.

The improvement in university outcomes was steep across the 2010s. Gen Z picked up the rate of progress from the Millennials and have maintained it since. It is also worth noting that the number of degrees awarded during the 2010s rose by almost 20%. This was despite the imposition of the higher tuition fee cap in England in 2010, which practically tripled fees to £9,000 per year. The increased number of undergraduates did not lead to a dilution in outcomes; in fact, it was the opposite.

While the percentage of upper second or better degrees has increased by approximately 50%, it is not the most impressive statistic. That belongs to the percentage of first-class degrees, which almost doubled over the course of the 2010s as Gen Z made their way through university.

There are a number of possible factors behind this, some of which have been better researched than others. They include the significantly increased costs of attending university, which led to undergraduates demanding more from their lecturers. When I started university in 1990, there were no tuition fees and the student grant was still commonplace. It was usual for students to live away from home, even with the additional costs of student accommodation. Students had debt, but my recollection is that it came from funding alcohol and other recreational habits. The idea of leaving university with a lifetime of debt despite not partying heavily every night was unthinkable.

The improvements in A level outcomes were not as significant as with university degrees, despite the fact that there has been far more media attention on the former. The reason for this attention is that the scene of school students opening their results together[1] and then going off to their respective universities makes for a good story. The same scene does not happen at universities.

In 2001, when the older Millennials were finishing their studies, 38% of grades were A or B. Six years later in 2007 (still Millennials), it was almost 10 points higher. The increase in the percentage of A grades led to the introduction of the A* grade so universities and employers were able to identify the best of the best. In the Gen Z years (2015 onwards), the now A* to B figure was 5 points higher again.

---

1   In modern times, A level results are not quite the surprise they used to be, as students can find out the status of their UCAS application from midnight on results day. The extent to which they have met, or not met, the requirements is what they see when they open their results. That is for those intending to go to university. Those who do not intend to go rarely feature in the media story.

It is also worth adding that it is possible, likely even, that over time a student can receive a worse grade despite having achieved a higher score in the examination, because grade boundaries have moved upwards. There is a lot more to this than can be described here. There is also an argument that 'exam factory' schools, a narrower curriculum, school accountability and teacher workload have also been contributory factors to a rise in outcomes.

GCSE outcomes are harder to measure over time because the entire grading system changed in 2017 (from A*-G to 9-1), and the qualifications permitted to count towards the main accountability measures changed a lot over the 2010s too. Both of these developments were made at least partly in response to grade inflation concerns. However, there is a similar pattern in terms of outcomes as seen with A levels.

For those who say that improvements in outcomes are down to grade inflation, parental pressure, school accountability measures and so on, I do understand this perspective to an extent. I am not arguing that Gen Z's gains are wholly down to their own diligence, just that it is genuine and the most significant contributory factor.

A survey of 13-17-year-olds in the USA published in *The Economist* in 2019 was entitled 'Generation Z is stressed, depressed and exam-obsessed'.[iii] I would say this tallies with my own experience of working with students in schools.

When asked what mattered to them most, the most popular answer by a distance was 'get good grades'. More than twice as many (almost 60%) said that this mattered 'a lot' compared to any other response, which included those relating to their appearance, being good at sport, being sexually active or consuming either alcohol or drugs (both very low on the list).

There have also been suggestions that the improvement in outcomes was artificial and was created as an incentive for students to attend particular universities. The university sector is sensitive to these claims, and understandably so. There's a case for saying both teaching and facilities improved, as did resources for learning through the digital revolution.[2]

I am not saying that any of these factors are totally fictitious or have had no impact. It is difficult to ignore an analysis that degree classifications have lost at least some of their value.[iv]

A multi-generational survey from Monster in the USA in 2016[v] showed an interesting dichotomy. Gen Z will work at unsociable times for higher pay, but also that salary is not everything. I should add the caveat that there is likely to be a time of life element here; having children can affect your answers to such questions. Having said that, the rise in the average age of the new parent, and the numbers who are not planning to have children, means there will be plenty of Millennials without children answering the survey, and there is a step-change in attitudes between these generations.

It could also be said that those from the older generations will have more skills and experience, which means they do not need to work anti-social hours. The fact they are more likely to own property and be more financially stable only reinforces that. In this light, the percentage of older generations prepared to work nights and weekends is arguably high.

---

2   University degree outcomes are regulated by the Office for Students. Given each university sets its own standards, it is a more unwieldy task than for schools. There are five exam boards across England, Wales and Northern Ireland, of which two are much smaller. WJEC focuses on Wales, and CCEA on Northern Ireland.

	Gen Z	Millennials	Gen X	Boomers
Responsible for driving own career	76	64	67	75
Motivated by money	70	63	59	59
Work should have a greater purpose than earning a salary	74	45	40	33
Willing to work nights and weekends for higher pay	58	45	40	33

Figure 13: Multi-generational survey, Monster

My point is that a so-called 'slack' generation who wanted to pick and choose their hours would not be prepared to work anti-social hours. In the same survey, 76% of Gen Z respondents described themselves as responsible for driving their own career. They know it is on them.

Gen Z should not be characterised or stereotyped as slackers. The extent to which they will uphold their personal values about, for example, equality or work-life balance should not be conflated with a reluctance to work hard. The educational outcomes, and the level of priority they give to them, show otherwise.

Demanding more

A further effect of the increased costs of going to university meant that students demanded more from themselves. I saw it for myself in the schools I led, and not just in the sixth form. Students stayed later, arrived earlier and took more work home with them. Their focus and desire to succeed grew. In addition, the messages about the combined impact of technological advances, an uncertain economy and globalisation on their future prospects cut through, and these had an impact on their sense of urgency.

There was also an increase in urgency amongst those who taught them. Expectations of what students could achieve, particularly those from less-privileged backgrounds, shifted. The Department for Education's focus on 'pupil premium'[3] students, in both published measures of examination performance and Ofsted inspections, did a lot to concentrate minds.

At the same time as pathways opened up to people from less-privileged backgrounds, results at university dispelled prejudices that increased access to university would 'naturally' lead to lower outcomes. If anything, the rate of educational progress shows those disadvantaged young people and those who speak English as an additional language are more likely to do well at university.

As the regulator Office for Students states: 'We believe the OfS must be careful not to assume that students with lower entry grades, typically from more disadvantaged backgrounds, cannot achieve first-class degrees.'

Changes in methodology mean it is harder to evaluate improvements at A level or GCSE. Having said that, some of the changes came as a result of wanting to avoid accusations of grade inflation. One of these was the introduction of the A* grade to A levels in 2010. As the percentage of A grades had increased so markedly, universities wanted a way of determining which were the best grades.

An A* grade was introduced to GCSEs in 1994, six years after their introduction, but the desire to distinguish the best 'top grades' and 'pass grades' was also a driver for the change from the A* to G

---

3   This referred to any student who either qualified for free school meals, or had done so at any point in the previous six years. This was an astute idea, as it captured the students whose family income might fluctuate either side of the line over a period of time.

methodology to 9 to 1 in 2017. The government wanted a distinction between a 'pass' and a 'good pass', but also wanted the top grade to be harder to attain. Furthermore, the grading methodology shifted, in effect, from 'criterion referenced' to 'norm referenced' when it was introduced for English and mathematics[vi]. The number who could 'pass' was fixed so it could not go up even if performance had improved. This left open the possibility, if not probability, that a student who would have passed in 2016 would not have done so two years later.[4]

Casual, but not slack

Gen Z's approach to working hard might be different to their predecessors, but that does not mean they are less interested in achieving high outcomes. Don't be fooled by what you think you see.

They value efficiency but not looking busy. Digital natives are more likely to invest time in automating repetitive tasks, rather than doing them manually because it fills the time. The same applies to using technology to streamline a workflow, or multitasking through the use of additional monitors. Given that personal appearance, including how they dress, is not a factor in whether a project will be successfully completed, they are less likely to value it and particularly to meet the standards of an older generation.

Gen Zers may have a stronger sense of when they are most productive, which could be outside a traditional 9 to 5 regime. They

---

4   Any educationalist reading this would likely prefer I add a little
     detail. English, English literature and mathematics were the first three
     of the new GCSEs in 2017. The methodology was that 'broadly the
     same proportion of students will achieve a grade 4 and above as
     currently achieve a grade C and above' and that 'broadly the same
     proportion of students will achieve a grade 7 and above as currently
     achieve an A and above'.

will communicate their availability and, by extension, when they are not available, during which time they may be getting deeper work done without interruption.

A preference for collaboration is borne from the synergies which emerge during the process, meaning that problems can be solved more quickly and without the need for an extended, structured meeting. For those running side hustles, they can bring experience and skills that cut through the detail and speed everything up.

Strategies to foster contribution

"Do you want to be a dictator? Do you only want to move from the top? Do you want an organisation that only lives, breathes, succeeds and dies by your word? If that's the case, then good luck to you, but there's no way to have a productive workforce if you do."

Gen Zer

As we dived into in Chapter 5, we live in an age of perennial, endless feedback. Comments are invited on every article and social media post. There are half a million comments posted per minute on Facebook alone.[vii] Your input is requested on every online purchase, printed on restaurant receipts and requested in one email after another.

Generation Z has grown up with this culture. Like everyone else, they may turn down the vast majority of opportunities to give their viewpoint, but when they do want to offer feedback, they expect to be able to do so. They are accustomed to giving input as to how something can work for them, in order to produce their best.

Leaders and their organisations are going to receive feedback from their youngest employees whether they ask for it or not.

Given this, they need to ensure those channels are open and well-advertised. Some leaders take a while to arrive at this position. I have CEO coaching clients who can be incredulous at receiving an unsolicited and informal email ('Hi FirstName!') from someone two weeks into their job who has various ideas about how the organisation as a whole could be improved.

"I wouldn't have dared to communicate with the boss directly in my first proper job at all, let alone that soon," they tell me. When I ask what they made of the ideas they received, it is pretty common that they have not even been read. A lot of time may have passed between that email arriving and any form of response. As far as that employee is concerned, you have ghosted them. Expect that word to spread.

This can feel deeply unsettling to a leader. No doubt, it is a paradigm shift. In general, leaders from older generations can get to a position where they understand why life has changed, and that the old way of doing things has to be reconsidered. The harder element is knowing what to do next. Managing expectations of young staff who may take some time to understand that life has changed, and to what degree, can also be challenging.

The old adage that if you want commitment from people then they need[viii] to be involved has never been more true. You have to make it clear that you welcome their input, no matter how much of it there might be and how often it might arrive. Without a sense of 'you-said-we-did', a lot of your potential future leaders will wander off very quickly, and often to a rival.

Even then, channels are not enough. **You have to go past welcoming whatever arrives to actively seeking it.** The town hall, the workshop, the survey, the working party are all key component parts. Despite how keen they may be to have their voices heard, some will not act unless prompted.

This is for two reasons. The first is that they feel shy in coming forward. That is not a Gen Z issue per se, although they may feel more apprehensive than those older generations. The second is that their expectation will be that they are asked, because everyone else asks them for their feedback. If your practice is not to reach out, it may take a while for your young staff to realise that they need to be proactive. By the time that happens, a lot of valuable points are likely to be lost.

If this is making you uncomfortable, then I am afraid my recommendation is to go even further. Every engagement makes a contribution towards your ability to retain. Your employees may well have chosen to apply to your organisation on the basis of your values and policies. **If they liked what they saw, there are benefits to asking them if their experience has lived up to what you advertised. If it has not, you need to find out why and how it can be different next time.**

You also need to ask them earlier than you might think is necessary. The act of asking will go a long way, even if they have not had an opportunity to form an opinion. They need to be told, and feel, that they matter from the very beginning. Those first impressions are not just vital, but precarious.

It could only be a single employee's perception, but it may also tell you something about your organisation, and the people in it, that you really needed to know. Just because they are not happy with everything does not mean they will instantly leave, but they are more likely to go sooner without an opportunity to express it. Every idea they have for you is a chance for you to demonstrate your responsiveness and that you are interested in their contributions.

You do not need to be available to everyone at all times to hear what your young employees have to say, but if you do not set some boundaries that is where this leads.

As I advocate elsewhere, be explicit about the boundaries. For example:

- When is your office door open or closed?
- Which issues should go to their manager and what should go to you?
- Are the feedback channels easy to find?
- Who replies and how long does it take to receive a response?
- Will everyone receive a response?
- Will others see your idea and what happened to it?

Communicate how you expect informal feedback to work too. If they see you next to the coffee machine, should they raise a topic or will you always tell them to send an email?

Strategies to communicate meaningful participation

Stating boundaries will not go far enough. **Part of your responsibility in encouraging contribution is to check that communication methods are known and understood by your employees.** If you have received nothing between bi-monthly town hall meetings, find out why. Perhaps your meetings are incredibly effective, but the feedback does not arrive, so you need to reconsider. The town hall is the opportunity to demonstrate that it is worth contributing, because you have the chance to say what you have done about it. If nothing is coming through, then either your communication channels are not well-advertised, not easy to use, or people think it is not worth bothering. Again, you need to find out the answer.

When you are clear in this way, and authentic about how you express it, not only will you receive the feedback your employees want to be able to provide, but you will also get the ideas you really need. They may be ideas that would not have come up around the C-suite table but add huge value. There may be others that gain traction with the workforce, or that tackle a potential side-effect which had not been anticipated but would be pricey to fix.

Explaining these benefits will also have a positive effect on your young employees. First, it is good for them to see that there was a positive benefit to the conversation they had. And second, it is an opportunity for you to explain the bigger picture and how different areas of the organisation interact. In effect, it is professional development for your staff.

An organisation that welcomes feedback enjoys the luxuries of avoiding the most expensive mistakes as well as having an alert workforce that buys into the idea they can shape its future direction. If you want to grow your own future leaders, what else could you start asking for? This is more than a feedback loop; it is about driving culture change, sharing skills and improving retention. It can be a wonderful tool for the multi-generational workplace.

Gen Z has a propensity to contribute, contrary to the Myth of Slack. If staff engagement ever was a bolt-on or tick-box, it is no longer the case. It really counts with your younger staff, and gives them the opportunity to shine. It needs to be central to what you do.

Your staff need to be engaged and to be kept engaged. At times, it may feel like you are sending a lot into the ether and that it may take too many prompts to get anything back. Unfortunately, that is part of life these days with ever greater competition to catch attention on social media feeds. It is really important to persist.

Let's look at some examples of levels of Gen Z engagement, starting with voting at UK general elections.

The 2015 UK general election was the first in which any Gen Z could vote. The oldest Gen Zs then found that two further opportunities to vote in general elections followed soon after in 2017 and 2019. I will go through the relevance of this in a moment.

Turnout fell from 2017 to 2019 in the five eldest age bands, but not for the youngest two. Turnout for 18-24-year-olds rose as more Gen Z became old enough to vote. By 2019, they form the majority of this age group.

It remains true that age is a significant factor and, overall, the older you are, the more likely you are to vote. However, by 2019, the pattern was fractured in that a higher proportion of Gen Z (majority 18-24) voted compared to the younger Millennials (almost all 25-35).

High levels of turnout have not been restricted to general elections. In the 2016 Brexit referendum, turnout for the under 25s (of which a large majority were still Millennials, but even so it reinforces the trend) was 64%, almost the same as it was for 40-54-year-olds at 66%.

I do not take these trends as an indication of support from Gen Z for their political institutions, but I do take it as evidence of their propensity to participate and use their voice in general. It is also a pragmatic step to hold on to whatever level of influence they can, given the extremely poor financial situation they have inherited. When meaningful and carefully constructed opportunities are put in front of Gen Z, the Myth of Slack fizzles out very quickly.

There is good evidence that both Millennials and Gen Zs are more likely to take particular kinds of action than previous generations at the same time of life. It is also more than possible that this will be a habit that sticks as they go through life, not least because the means of doing so in this day and age makes it far easier.

While the ease of making a contribution has led to accusations that electronic activism is actually 'slacktivism' or 'clicktivism', any effort is still a contribution. As any social media marketeer knows, even a single click or comment can be highly prized. The vast majority of posts and emails do not receive a click, no matter who they are from. Campaigners seek engagement in the form of clicks and comments, because they generate more views from the social media algorithms. One click can lead to someone seeing it, who otherwise would not, who in turn might make a financial contribution to a campaign.

The percentage of posts that any typical Gen Z user interacts with, rather than scrolls past, is tiny. The number of emails received each day is very small compared to the number of social media posts seen, and the click-to-open rate. Stopping and reading a post, or watching a video, may also seem small, but represents a greater level of commitment than what is given to the vast majority. Gen Zs are also very aware that even watching a TikTok video to the end not only represents relatively strong engagement, but is also giving some data to the algorithm, in turn influencing their future experience on the platform.

I am not claiming that every click or like means that a post or video has been carefully considered before action is taken. Doubtless many posts are supported without reading or watching the whole thing. There is no evidence that Gen Z is guilty of that more than any other generation. On the contrary, Gen Z is painfully aware of the value of their 'watch history' to others, and the implication of every click they take. Electronic activism may require little effort, but it can still be highly effective and be the result of advanced filtering techniques at speed. Gen Z understands the power of this more than anyone else.

Social media engagement is also only one example of participation. There is a wider picture that supports the argument for Gen Z as strong contributors.

Deloitte's 2022 survey showed statistics for different forms of participation or, as they describe it, 'taking action to drive the change they want to see in the world'. The survey focuses on 11 categories and compares the outcomes of Millennials and Gen Z. The latter is ahead in nine categories, level in one and behind in the only one that requires them to make a financial commitment (donating to charity).

Categories where Gen Z is ahead included:

- Choosing their type of work based on personal ethics.
- Volunteering.
- Creating social media content relating to social issues.
- Raising money.
- Attending public meetings.
- Campaigning.
- Contacting elected representatives.

Of course, there are factors in play for each cohort that impact their ability to participate. The opportunity may be greater when you are at a stage of life with more time on your hands; for example, before parenthood, which applies to more of Gen Z here. As I have said elsewhere, the need for multiple sources of income to pay the bills also acts as a severe drain on time, which tips the scale the other way. Many members of Gen Z have less time on their hands for that reason. Furthermore, the large majority of the tasks above can be carried out without leaving the house, which levels the playing field.

The two areas in which Gen Z is furthest ahead are also the ones that require the biggest time commitments: volunteering and campaigning.

This is further evidence of their commitment to their values, and perhaps also towards altruism.

These activities show Gen Z's propensity to contribute to the success of their organisations if given the opportunity. A greater tendency to attend public meetings, run campaigns and create content not only shows an inclination to contribute, but also a set of skills that can be utilised to good effect in the workplace, including in management positions. It is another example of how savvy leaders can use Gen Z's knowledge, skills and aptitudes beyond work to their advantage. This is a win-win.

Organisations will help themselves if they draw attention to that connection. The young staff who may be too introverted to put their hand up in a staff meeting may be presenting plenty of evidence about their potential leadership qualities. Gen Z's desire to participate is only part of the story. The brands, influencers and organisations that matter to them have reached their level partly through the engagement of others. A company that does not value contributions or collaboration will neither be seen as one they should want to join, nor one that is likely to thrive.

Endnotes

i   OfS. (2024). *Analysis of degree classifications over time.* https://www.officeforstudents.org.uk/media/gzcftkrn/analysis-of-degree-classifications-over-time-2024.pdf

ii   Wikipedia contributors. (2025, March 9). *British undergraduate degree classification.* Wikipedia. https://en.wikipedia.org/wiki/British_undergraduate_degree_classification#/media/File:United_Kingdom_degree_classification_trends_line_chart.png

iii   The Economist. (2019b, February 27). Generation Z is stressed, depressed and exam obsessed. *The Economist.* https://www.economist.com/graphic-detail/2019/02/27/generation-z-is-stressed-depressed-and-exam-obsessed

iv   Lambert, H. (2023, February 7). The great university con: how the British degree lost its value. *New Statesman.* https://www.newstatesman.com/politics/2019/08/the-great-university-con-how-the-british-degree-lost-its-value

v   Monster. (n.d.). Move over, millennials: What you'll need to know for hiring as Gen Z enters the workforce. In *Monster Multi-Generational Survey.* https://www.monstergovernmentsolutions.com/docs/misc/monster_genz_report.pdf

vi   Ofqual. (2014, November 27). Setting standards for new GCSEs in 2017. *GOV.UK.* https://www.gov.uk/government/news/setting-standards-for-new-gcses-in-2017

vii   Marino, S. (2025, January 17). *What happens in an internet minute: 90+ fascinating online stats.* LocaliQ. https://localiq.com/blog/what-happens-in-an-internet-minute/#:~:text=Facebook%20statistics&text=Facebook%20users%20are%20still%20incredibly,Instagram%2C%20Whatsapp%2C%20etc

viii   Covey, S. R. (1997). *The Seven Habits of Highly Effective People.* Macmillan Reference USA.

8

The Myth of Fake

"Generation Z workers are terrifying their Millennial bosses with a series of woke and entitled demands, including that their companies support Black Lives Matter, provide paid time off for 'anxiety', and telling the CEOs to do the assignments themselves.

These newest additions to the workforce have left many of their not-much-older supervisors shaking their heads or infuriated before caving in to avoid social media shaming by the web-savvy 'dot-com kids'."

Daily Mail [i]

If you are familiar with the British press, you might roll your eyes at the sight of a *Daily Mail* story. I may have done the same if it was the only reference. As the culture wars took hold on social media, I started to hear similar comments through various media outlets, on TV, on the radio and in other newspapers. Worse still, and as you know by now, I heard it amongst my peers.

I do not have a precise timeline, but I remember a period when use of the phrase 'politically correct' had died out and before 'woke' was in common usage. This was in the early 2010s when the Conservative-led coalition was in government, Labour was out and the London Olympics brought a nation together.[i]

The origins of the word 'woke' were covered in Matthew Syed's 2023 BBC Radio 4 series.[ii] Although he found examples of its modern use in both the 1930s and 1960s, it took off in 2014. This followed the shooting of Black teenager Michael Brown in Missouri, USA. Brown was killed by a white police officer and his death sparked weeks of unrest. The phrase #staywoke became prevalent on Twitter in particular in order to encourage people to remain aware of the threat of systemic racism. In other words, stay alert.

As time went on, the phrase 'identity politics'[2] became more popular. This also became associated with wokeness and the word 'woke' was increasingly used as an insult, particularly after Donald Trump was first elected President of the United States in 2016 and the Conservative Party moved to the right in seeking to 'Get Brexit Done'.

As a result of woke being a mainstream insult hurled at Gen Z, I did consider calling this chapter the 'Myth of Woke' or combining fake and woke together. In the end, I decided that the culture war element of woke would be a distraction from the main arguments. It is true that people who hold so-called woke opinions and positions are

---

1   You might view this as hyperbole, but I'm genuine about this. The nation, and perhaps more pertinently its press, were on board. It felt like we had moved past a difficult period. Sigh.

2   Defined as 'political or social activity by or on behalf of a racial, ethnic, cultural, religious, gender, or other group, usually undertaken with the goal of rectifying injustices suffered by group members because of differences or conflicts between their particular identity (or misconceptions of their particular identity) and the dominant identity (or identities) of a larger society'. Thank you, Brittanica.com.

accused of not doing so genuinely; the second criticism is that there is a performative aspect to holding them. Fake carries a broader definition beyond politics and culture. For the purpose of this chapter, I will deal with woke as a subset of fake, and refer to it only minimally.

Workplace observations

As you might expect, I am about to counter both of these arguments, but first I will spell out what I hear and read. Let's take a look at the kinds of ideas I see Gen X sharing about Gen Z.

- "They make their minds up so quickly on a topic based on a little scrolling and what one or two people have said. There is a reluctance to think things through for themselves. They are overly concerned with social and cultural issues that do not affect them, and the next bandwagon to jump on. It is all so superficial."
- "'Cancel culture' is a problem. I do not care what anyone says. Somebody said something in the office that they didn't like. They shouldn't have said it and, to be fair, it took them a minute to realise why it was a problem. It also took far too long for the younger staff to realise why they may not have known why it was a problem."
- "I see how some of them portray themselves on social media and it worries me. They use all these filters to look completely different, and portray themselves in that light. It is as though how they look is not enough. It is hard to convince them otherwise."
- "They can be completely intolerant of other perspectives or views. That's the problem with social media; it can just be an echo chamber. When someone makes a point that does not fit in with theirs, they can be very animated and then want to shut the conversation down."
- "The environment matters, and I agree that it is important to stop climate change, but it also comes at a cost, which they do not want to know about. It is also hard to hear about this when they

are constantly buying and returning clothes, and their dinner arrives on a moped."

- "The word 'triggered' comes out so quickly, and they do go from 0 to 100 at even the slightest issue. It gets overused, feels practised even. Unintentional slights are interpreted as deliberate offences. It can make them very difficult to talk to. We might not live in their world, but they do not want to meet us halfway. Tolerance appears to apply to everyone apart from us."

- "If some people do not want to state their 'preferred pronouns', I do not expect them to be hassled for it. Yet it seems to be a baseline expectation for so many. The older staff do not understand identity politics, and I do not see that they should have to."

- "There is a lot that presents as hypocritical to me. They are not short of telling me about their rights and the limits of their contract, but then they go home and order food that requires a zero-hours worker with no employment protections to deliver it to them."

- "Some seem to think that the higher the number of social media followers, the more true it must be. The same applies to five star reviews. They are not prepared to dig beneath the surface."

- "All of this leads to a duller workplace when we can only talk about work. It undercuts why spending some days together in the office is important."

An autonomous generation

Before covering another key characteristic and strategies for employers, let's dig a little deeper into how Gen Z's views are not homogenous.

In the 2024 general election in the UK, polls generated at least as much news as policy analysis. Partly, this was because poll after poll indicated a Labour landslide which seemed unrealistic, and partly it was because at one point it seemed possible that the Conservatives may not even form the opposition.

The Conservative Party's status as one of the two main parties was at threat partly because of the performance of the Reform Party[3], which was already polling well even before Nigel Farage took back the leadership and said he would be running for a seat.

Reform's voting base is closely related to the Brexit referendum of 2016, not least because of the impact Farage had on the result. In the referendum, a majority of older voters chose to leave the European Union, and a majority of younger voters to stay. As is often the case with psephology, outcomes are rarely so binary. At least 55% of all age groups over 45 voted to leave and 73% of 18-24 to stay. Very few Gen Zs were old enough to vote.

After Farage entered the general election race in 2024, opinion polls showed some changes. Reform first gained ground on the Conservatives and then drew level. Then Conservative MP Jacob Rees-Mogg referred to the Conservative and Reform vote as a single group, which had divided over time. Opinion polling indicated a more complex position, showing that Reform's voters would be coming from a mixed audience across the political spectrum.

The position with age was different. In a mid-June poll from Redfield and Wilton, Labour was well ahead with 18-24-year-olds with a projected 51% of the vote. Only two weeks later, there was a significant change amongst 18-24-year-olds. Labour's projected vote had dropped by seven percentage points to 44% and Reform was a clear second with 15%.[4] The six percentage points it was above the Liberal Democrats and Greens may not seem like a lot,

---

3   I could have chosen the Liberal Democrats, or the wider theme of tactical voting for those who wanted 'anyone but a Conservative candidate'.

4   They were third amongst the Millennials in the 35-44 age bracket with 13%.

but comparatively Reform had two-thirds more support than either of them at the time. The Conservatives trailed behind with 7%.

It is true that both Farage and Reform had made significant gains in terms of the size of their social media audience, particularly on TikTok, but that does not necessarily lead to poll numbers, votes or seats in the House of Commons. The final election came out differently, although not just for the Reform party.[iii] Analysis shows that both Labour and Reform did not perform as highly amongst 18 to 24 years as opinion polls had shown, although the latter still did better than the outgoing Conservatives.

The main point I am making is that Gen Z is not a homogeneous group voting solely on green issues and identity politics. There is a libertarian streak, arguably more so than with the Millennials. The Labour government elected in 2024 will have to work hard to win over the youth vote given that a smaller percentage of those aged 18-24 (41%) voted Labour than 25-34 year-olds (47%). More voted for Reform than the Conservatives in both of these Gen Z relevant age groups.

In the 2024 US Presidential election, Harris may have beaten Trump amongst 18-29-year-olds overall, but it was close.[5] The gender gap was very significant amongst the under 30s as Trump was ahead with men by 14% and Harris with women by 18%.

There was a very considerable shift between the votes of the 'young' in 2020 (when Trump lost) and in 2024 (when he won). A higher percentage of young women and men voted for Trump in 2024 than had done so four years earlier when Biden was the opponent.

---

5   I am making an assumption that relatively equal numbers of men and women voted, and that the number of young voters who identify as non-binary would not have overturned any difference. Even if I'm wrong, it would not be a clear win for Harris.

I do not wish to overdo[6] the political analysis, but again the evidence points away from a homogenous group with a voting bloc for the left of their country's politics.[7] I will make a connection with Chapter 4 in that a lot of young people across the UK and USA in 2024 made pragmatic choices about politicians who they saw as most likely to benefit them economically, or did not participate at all if they did not see a party or a leader who would.

A diverse generation

"We have inherited some amazing things like the freedom to be ourselves. The generations before us fought for such important rights and provided us with a space to be ourselves. We can be queer and I'm grateful for that."

Gen Z member

Demonstrating that Gen Z is more diverse than previous generations is a straightforward task. Let's start by looking at ethnicity over the last three censuses in England and Wales.[8] Below are some statistics from the 2021 England and Wales census.[9] I acknowledge these 'high-level groupings' form extremely broad headings, not least 'Other', but they provide a starting point.

---

6   Actually I do, given my background in studying and teaching government and politics. But I'm not going to.

7   Although it is a common perception that the 'young vote left', voting behaviour is rarely that straightforward. Even in the Labour landslide from the 1997 general election, over a quarter of younger votes went to the Conservatives (Ipsos Mori). Only 8% voted for a party other than Conservatives, Labour or Liberal Democrat, less than a quarter of the estimated figure for the 2024 general election.

8   Chosen because Scotland carried out their census a year later.

9   England and Wales only because Scotland delayed its census for a year during the Covid-19 pandemic.

	2001	2011	2021	% change in 20 years
Asian	4.8%	7.5%	9.3%	up 94%
Black	2.2%	3.4%	4.0%	up 81%
Mixed	1.4%	2.2%	2.9%	up 107%
White British	87.4%	80.5%	74.4%	down 15%
Other	4.2%	6.4%	9.4%	up 124%

Figure 14: Percentage of England and Wales by high level ethnic groups 2001-2021[iv]

'White British' remains the largest group, but the percentage of those who are not in this group doubled in 20 years. The overall population grew[10] during this period, so although the 'White British' population shrank as a percentage, numbers remained stable across the whole period.

The percentage changes across this 20-year period in the other categories are relatively similar, although there is a significant difference in terms of numbers, given that 'Mixed' has fewer than a third as many people as 'Asian' or 'Other'.[11] On average, the percentage change of high-level groups other than 'White British' was around 100%; in other words, it doubled.

Population size changes for two reasons. The first is a difference

---

10   The total population in England and Wales was 52.3 million in 2001 and 59.6 million in 2021.

11   Given I was a headteacher in schools where 'any other ethnic group' (a large subset of 'other') was one of the biggest groups, I should spell it out. Groups who come under this category include Arab, Latin/South/Central American, Iranian, and Kurdish. Kurdish in itself might refer to Turkish, Iraqi, Syrian and Iranian. The 'any other' group also saw the fastest growth between 2011 and 2021, almost tripling from a third of a million in 10 years.

between the number of births and deaths; the second is the difference between those immigrating and emigrating. The population of England and Wales grew by 6.3% between 2011 and 2021, approximately 3.5 million people. The Office of National Statistics[v] estimates show that across this period 7.4 million immigrated and 5.2 million emigrated, leaving a net migration at 2.2 million. This accounts for approximately two-thirds of the population increase.[12]

The graphs below give some insight into what is happening with the other third. On average, the White British population is older; therefore, a smaller proportion of them are having children than other groups and a higher proportion are dying.

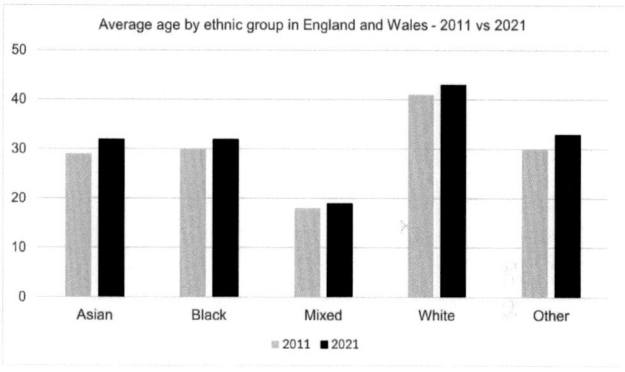

Figure 15: Average age of ethnic group – 2011 vs 2021 census in England and Wales

The average age for 'White British' is more than twice the age for 'Mixed', and approximately 25% older than the rest.

---

12   For those who thought Brexit would 'resolve' the issue, particularly fans of Boris Johnson, note that net migration in 2022 (the year he stepped down as Prime Minister) was over 872,000 and estimates for 2023 are 866,000. Both figures are several times higher than the net average from 2011 to 2021. 2.2 million over 10 years is 220,000.

The composition in classrooms is changing, as I saw from my own experience. The make-up of friendship groups changed in those classrooms too, and some of that is borne out by the increased number of those with 'Mixed' ethnicity. Not only are those with 'Mixed' ethnicity less than half the age of both the 'White British' and the overall population[13], but they are also the approximate average age of Gen Z.

Put simply, a key reason why ethnic diversity matters a great deal to Generation Z is because they are more diverse as a group. Given this, it is not a surprise that Gen Z feels passionately about discrimination. They are advocating for themselves.

According to a 2020 survey of Gen Zs by Tallo[14], 77% have seen discrimination and 51% have felt discriminated against on the basis of 'gender, ethnic, racial identity'. These are significant numbers, particularly as it does not take all types of discrimination into account. Across the focus groups, I found feelings ran high on the topic, not least because the idea of discriminating against anyone else on the basis of who they are or how they look makes no sense to them. Why would they discriminate against themselves or their friends?

Here is one example of those feelings, as expressed by a member of a Gen Z focus group.

> "I'm biracial, but also I've got a lot lighter skin than my sister, who's also biracial. I've definitely experienced people questioning my ethnicity growing up. They say 'where are you from?' I say, 'Oh, I grew up here'. Then they say, 'No,

---

13   The median age in the 2021 census in England and Wales was 40.

14   The Tallo survey was a global survey from a website which 'enables students to showcase themselves and be discovered by employers'.

but where are you actually from?'[15] *I just have no answer to that."*

Friends made online have further amplified the strength of feelings around diversity. One in four Gen Z would have to travel by plane to spend time in person with most of their friends from social media. That was before the pandemic.

Another focus group member referred to the older generation's use of social media as "emboldening them to say what they like totally unhindered". She referred to someone asking for a 'white nurse' to take her bloods in a hospital and becoming aggressive when it looked like that might not happen

If there is a single set of statistics that shows changes over time most effectively, it is this one. The percentage of the population who consider themselves to be exclusively heterosexual has dropped very significantly from one generation to the next.

Research by Ipsos Mori in 2020[vi] showed that 54% of Gen Z considered themselves to be 'exclusively heterosexual', compared to 66% for Millennials, 76% for Gen X and 81% for Baby Boomers. Across the space of a few decades, the numbers who do not consider themselves to be exclusively heterosexual has more than doubled.[16]

---

15   I am not going to go into details around microaggressions here, other than to say for the Gen Z groups I spoke to it is not a contradiction in terms. Also, phrases like 'where are you *actually* from?' are right up there as a roll-your-eyes problem.

16   There have been various surveys on this topic, including the 2021 census and no two surveys say the same thing, or necessarily ask quite the same question. There is a difference between 'who do you identify as' and whether they identify exclusively. I have seen both higher and lower figures than the 66% quoted above.

Referring back to the quote at the start of this chapter, it is not only the sexuality statistics where I have found gratitude for what Gen Z has inherited, accompanied by a determination to drive this through. As the eldest Gen Z enters their thirties, the decade of their life when they are most likely to become parents, my expectation is that will be carried through to their children and likely amplified further.

This poll found that 10% of Generation Z regards prejudice toward the LGBT community as one of the most pressing issues in the world today, as compared to only 2% of Millennials, Gen X, and Baby Boomers who believe the same. This underlines that diversity is not just more important to Gen Z because they are more diverse. They really believe in its significance and expect others to do the same.

Gen Z also sees itself as more broad-minded. The trend towards gender-neutral clothing is just one example. There is also the 'cancel culture' argument to say that Gen Z is a lot less tolerant about intolerance. I do not see this as an irony. Values count, and Gen Z expects to see the same from their employers.

Gen Z needs to see that commitments to diversity, equality and inclusion on an organisation's website are tangible in practice, not least in terms of representation. A business that does not take this seriously can expect their recruitment, retention and motivation issues to be that much more significant.

Strategies to show you value authenticity

"Pay is a factor in whether I stay in a job or not, but it is not the only one. The values of the organisation need to mean something to me, and I need to see them in practice. Otherwise they are just words."

Gen Zer

I have left one of the most important points of this book until last. For Gen Z, authenticity is everything. It is authenticity, allied with transparency, which will lead the best of the youngest generation in the workplace to give you a second look. Just as significantly, it is also authenticity that will give you the best chance of retaining those you spent so long recruiting.

Lots of organisations I have come across while putting together this book refer to 'integrity' as a core value. When I talk about authenticity and transparency to audiences, there can be an assumption that integrity is the same thing. I would argue that integrity has been overused to the point of it being a cliche. Organisations that use integrity as a core value may arouse a lot of suspicion, for fear they have not put in the groundwork to justify their claim. Therefore, integrity can appear a hollow claim. Unless it has come from a groundswell of opinion in a staff engagement exercise, and it is built on a foundation of both transparency and authenticity backed up by your workforce, I would steer clear.

After a talk I did, I was present at a roundtable discussion where a member of the group said: "We need to stop using the word 'integrity' on all our websites in huge white letters on a black background. It does not mean anything, and our young clients see through it." The group took a minute to absorb her words, but no one disagreed. You really have to 'be' something in order to claim it. The point particularly resonates for Gen Z, for whom words alone mean nothing. It is not that integrity does not matter. It really does. Yet it requires a much higher standard of proof today.

It is no longer good enough for an organisation's marketing to display only the best elements of what it does and who it is. Gen Z needs to see you for who you are as a basis for trust, whether you want to show it or not. 'Glossy' marketing used to feel professional; now it presents as duplicitous.

The percentage of Gen Z who 'expect to leave their job' in the short to medium term (18-24 months) has been around 50% for some years.[vii] It peaked at around 60% in the year immediately prior to the pandemic. As the lockdowns took hold, the case for staying put was strengthened, particularly if their job was furloughed and assuming the job still existed. The figures are higher for Gen Z than any other generation and a higher Gen Z attrition rate will be a bigger problem for companies than any other generation, because unlike all other generations, the number of Gen Zs in the workplace continues to grow.

It is conceivable that numbers of those who expect to leave for pastures new would rise in each passing year, as the older Gen Zs establish themselves professionally and have more to offer new employers. They also have more to offer themselves, as the skills and experience gained from employment can be used to set up their own organisations. While it is conceivable, the evidence does not yet point this way. Partly, that is because surveys do not typically divide Gen Z into subcategories.

The percentage of Gen Zers expecting to leave their jobs is far higher than those who do. The average turnover rate in the UK is 15%[viii]. The percentage of other generations who 'expect to leave' is also far higher than the 15% turnover rate (29% for Boomers, 28% for Gen X and 38% for Millennials). **In this climate, organisations need to adopt an approach that, first, they should always be retaining and, second, retention begins on day one of employment. This is primarily for Gen Z but the older generations too.**

The phrase 'expecting to leave' might mean that an employee is actively and perpetually looking for their next best option, or it could mean that they expect their organisation to let them go as an individual or as part of a larger change. In simple terms, an employee leaves an organisation for one of three reasons:

1. They are successful in applying for another job and leave for another employer.
2. They no longer wish to be employed because they are taking time out, retiring or setting up their own enterprise.
3. The organisation instigates their departure, whether through redundancy, a failed probationary period or other human resources procedure, or because they merge, reduce in size, or fold completely.

In this section, I will focus on the idea that it may not be through choice that approximately half of Gen Z expect to have a new employer in the short to medium term.

For a start, if job cuts have to be made (and plenty were during the pandemic, for example), the cheapest way of doing so is to adopt a 'last in, first out' approach. The newest members of staff also have a probationary period that they might not pass, particularly if organisations take on more staff than they need to fill the roles available with the expectation that many will not get through their probation.

There is also the point that 'expecting to leave' is only an indication. For many reasons, the employee might not do so. The better offer might not come along. The side hustle may not flourish as intended.

Even if employees do decide to stay for these reasons, there remains an opportunity for the employee to address some issues. While there might be costs associated with retaining employees, whether as an increase in salary or other benefits, the costs of recruiting from scratch dwarfs those retention costs. From the Gen Z employee's side, a job that allows for the cost of living to be met, and one that does not quite do that, may reflect a relatively small difference in salary but have a much greater psychological impact.

Employees' trust that they will be retained is not what it was either, particularly for young staff. Covid cuts hit the youngest first and hits them the hardest. Changes in employment practices, such as the move to zero-hour contracts within the gig economy, tend to affect Gen Z more than any other age group too. Contracting out has a much greater impact on the shop floor, and the lowest paid, than at director level, so that is something to bear in mind.

Retention rates are not uniform across industries. In fact, they can vary wildly and I have seen various figures over the course of this research. In 2021, Deloitte reported that the numbers of those who 'expected to leave' their job within two years was almost 20% higher in 'consumer' than 'health care'. The question asked only about jobs, rather than industries, so it is possible that someone could intend to leave their job but remain in the industry, or not. The percentage of Gen Zs who expected to move on were around 50% higher than Millennials on average.

The lack of correlation between Gen Z and Millennials is intriguing. The lowest of these five examples for Millennials were the highest two for Gen Z. However, I am far more interested in the variation within industries than across them, and therefore looking at the strategies individual organisations can use to retain their staff. Particular industries may have issues about, for example, convincing potential staff they have a future as the influence of artificial intelligence grows ever stronger. That aside, it is possible for a company in any industry to have lower turnover rates than its rivals and get it right when others get it wrong.

The key to retaining Gen Z staff is that, on appointment, they find the company culture and their role to be as described. Authenticity counts because the battle for retention starts as soon as your Gen Z employees arrive and does not let up.

Strategies to support transparency

There is a catch with this. What you think you described may not be what they heard. In addition, what you took for granted they would know may be news to them.

Remember the survey that stated less than 30% of young people in secondary school had access to work experience? On average, your new employees have much less experience of work than you did at the same stage. What might be obvious to you as a Gen Xer about the workplace is not obvious to Gen Z. Plenty of them may have been working on their own projects, including buying and selling online, but done from their bedroom and not in a workplace.

The same can apply to moving from a virtual workplace to a physical one. The shift from a series of calls over the course of the day at home, punctuated by periods of time not surrounded by your colleagues, to not being able to escape them can be pretty dramatic, particularly if it is for the first time.

If you want to recruit high-quality members of this generation, you also need to think hard about who does the describing and in what format. Gen Z has spent their lives surrounded by clickbait. It takes longer to convince them of the truth of what you are saying. Be prepared to be asked the same question in different ways, for all you say to be double-checked and verified elsewhere, and to defend yourself against online rumour and Glassdoor[17] reviews. It may reassure you that Gen Z will also be far more perceptive than you

---

17   If you have not looked this up, I recommend you do. If you cannot face that, ask someone to do it for you. If it is in the public domain on a popular website, you should know about it. The same applies to Google reviews. It might be desirable to ignore all online activity, but there can be a genuine impact on your reputation.

might realise in filtering out messages from aggrieved ex-employees they are grateful not to have to work with. They are likely to have read more 'bad review for effect' comments than you have.

Text on a website only goes so far. In fact, websites themselves only go so far for three reasons. The first is that this is your version of events, packaged to present your business in the best possible light. While new content may appear in the forms of blogs and podcasts, they are relatively static. Secondly, social media channels offer an organisation opportunities to communicate regularly and to reach prospective staff without them requesting it, whether through organic reach or advertising. Thirdly, and perhaps most importantly, social media channels are full of images and videos that are far more likely to cut through than words in black and white.

Video is the most effective method as it conveys the greatest level of transparency. You get to see and hear the people who are promoting the job, along with their body language and tone of voice. You can work out a lot of information from a 30-second video.

It may be possible for artificial intelligence tools to manufacture video testimonials from allegedly recently recruited staff in the same way as is possible on the printed page. I would not advise it as a tactic. As time goes on, people start to work out which images, video and audio is fake and what is real. Promoting something fake is reputationally disastrous when discovered, which is, in my view, inevitable. You might have to work harder than you imagine to persuade Gen Z that the testimonial video is real. The more artificial intelligence enables new possibilities, the more the youngest generation in the workplace wants to see and feel something human.

You need to go further than you might feel reasonable in terms of being open and transparent. Better still, go to the point of

presenting your vulnerabilities. You may get a stronger response than you imagine from saying 'these are our weaknesses and this is how you can help'. You are likely to find that opening up about problems piques interest, implying that the role is something more than coming in at the bottom of an organisation. When your new employees arrive, they may well ask how they can get started with resolving those issues. They will not expect to be confined to 'bottom of the pile' work if they have been promised otherwise.

Being who you say you are also means repeating it, ad nauseum. The phrase 'everyone singing from the same hymn sheet' may be a cliché, but generating trust means that your new Gen Z staff do hear those values and key messages expressed from a variety of sources. It needs to feel natural and not forced though, otherwise you will not generate the desired levels of authenticity.

If you feel the key messages are expressed too often, that is likely to be something you notice more than they do. This generation is very used to the repetition of messages. If they stop coming, they may wonder why and what the implications are. Those implications could be that you did not mean what you originally said, or that those messages no longer apply because new ones now apply and you do not intend to communicate them. It might sound far-fetched to you, but it will resonate with your Gen Z staff.

Maintaining the narrative of where your organisation is going, why it is going there and how really matters. When it looks as though you need to change course, say why early on. Connecting the workforce to decisions made at the centre offers a great deal of reassurance. Keep bringing the core messages to life as you do, and ensure others do the same.

As you communicate change, ensure the invitation for comment and challenge is firmly open. This not only reinforces transparency and authenticity, but it empowers your colleagues to find the holes in your argument you had not spotted. It can be very powerful for a young member of staff to feel they can say what others had identified but did not want to raise. Far better that they do this before those messages go into the public domain with your customer base.

It is so much harder in the modern age for messages to cut through amongst the noise of the thousands of marketing messages everyone encounters every day. It is at least as difficult to pull one back that does cut through, but which you did not intend. Your challenge is not only to ensure key messages do get out, but also to keep them live once they have. In fact, you may not achieve the former with your Gen Z staff until you have done the latter.

As already established in this chapter, Gen Z is more diverse than their predecessors. They will also quickly spot an organisation that claims to prize equity, diversity and inclusion but that has a top table indicating the opposite. Even if the composition of your top table has not got that far, it will mean something to recognise this and articulate what you are doing about it, along with the impact you would like it to have. Again, establish this as an issue where you need Gen Z's help.

If you want to recruit and retain effectively, Gen Z needs to see that you mean what you say. If you say diversity, for example, matters to you, then demonstrate that on Gen Z's terms. Your commitment to diversity and inclusion needs to be seen and heard in actions and outcomes. It is not difficult to 'commit' to anything, but designing processes and challenging mindsets that have a palpable impact takes time and effort. You might think it's not worth expressing this to the outside world, but I would recommend you do. It shows that you mean what you say and offers a valuable additional layer of public accountability.

This should be considered an investment. In today's climate, it will make a highly significant difference in your ability to recruit and retain the best Gen Z talent. Being who you say you are does not happen overnight. Demonstrating the journey you intend to follow to get there will only help you on your way.

The irony about the Myth of Fake is that Gen Z themselves are hardest to persuade that something is genuine. Organisations that bend over backwards to demonstrate they are who they say they are put themselves in the best possible position to recruit and retain the best.

Endnotes

i   Coulter, C. (2021, November 1). Gen-Z workers are terrifying their millennial bosses with woke demands. *Mail Online.* https://www. dailymail.co.uk/news/article-10149905/Gen-Z-workers-terrifying-millennial-bosses-woke-demands.html

ii   *BBC Radio 4 – Woke: The Journey of a Word – Available now.* (2023b, February 24). BBC. https://www.bbc.co.uk/programmes/ m001jc1l/episodes/player

iii Ipsos Mori. (2024, July 26) *How Britain voted in the 2024 general election.* https://www.ipsos.com/en-uk/how-britain-voted-in-the-2024-election

iv   Garlick, S. (2022, November 29). *Ethnic group, England and Wales – Office for National Statistics.* https://www.ons.gov. uk/peoplepopulationandcommunity/culturalidentity/ethnicity/ bulletins/ethnicgroupenglandandwales/census2021

v   Tammes, P. (2023, November 23). *Estimating UK international migration: 2012 to 2021 – Office for National Statistics.* https://www.ons.gov.uk/peoplepopulationandcommunity/ populationandmigration/internationalmigration/articles/ estimatingukinternationalmigration2012to2021/2023-11-23

vi   Ipsos Mori. (2020, June 26) *Sexual orientation and attitudes to LGBTQ+ in Britain.* https://www.ipsos.com/en-uk/sexual-orientation-and-attitudes-lgbtq-britain

vii *50% of Gen Z workers think about leaving their job – HRZone.* (2023, December 30). HRZone. https://hrzone.com/blog/50-of-gen-z-workers-think-about-leaving-their-job/#:~:text=Employees%20 were%20asked%20if%20they,25%2D39)%2038%25

viii Hiring UK EN Merchandise. (2010, June 11). *What is the ideal employee turnover rate? | Monster.co.uk.* https://www.monster. co.uk/advertise-a-job/resources/workforce-management-planning/employee-retention-strategies/what-is-the-ideal-employee-turnover-rate/

PART THREE

LOOKING TO THE FUTURE

9

What Does the Future Hold for Gen Z?

Speculation is an imprecise science. Recent history has led me to be wary of trajectories.

If I had been told almost 20 years ago when I took up post as a headteacher that despite all the incredible (as it seemed at the time) new technology coming through, the UK's issues with poverty would become so much worse in the decades to follow, I would not have believed it. In 15 years, the number of users of food banks has increased from 25,000 to over 3 million[i], a staggering and shameful figure. The same applies to the pandemic, which I assumed was a topic to learn about in history books. I had seen too many health panics come and go to take Covid-19 seriously at the start.

I also thought the kind of extreme right-wing politics expressed by the BNP, National Front and worse had disappeared. I was as bewildered as anyone by John McCain's choice of Sarah Palin as his running mate in the 2008 US Presidential election and did not foresee this as a forerunner of Trumpian politics or where the UK's national government would end up between the Brexit vote and the 2024 general election.

Maybe those examples say too much about me. Even so, the case remains that the past and present are unreliable guides to the future. Advances in technology may create a stack of possibilities, but just because something can happen does not mean that it will. There has been enough food and water for everyone on earth even throughout the population explosion of the last 100 years, yet it does not guarantee distribution.

And so, even if every predication I make here about Gen Z and Gen Alpha leaves me hostage to fortune, I'm sharing some of my well-informed guesses. One thing is certain. Much unpredictability lies ahead and Gen Z will have to keep adapting the best they can. The same applies to Gen Alpha, the large majority of whom are already born, and the eldest making their way through secondary school.

Below are six predictions for Gen Z as the rest of cohort becomes eligible to join the workplace and the older half (the focus of this book so far) head into their thirties and beyond.

1. Portfolio careers will become the norm

Given the focus of this book, the world of work is the most obvious place to start. Traditional career paths will still exist, but fewer Gen Z will pursue them. The ability to hop from project to project, job to job will only become more popular. The same applies to the 'fractional' career, where an individual carries out the same work for a variety of employers.[1] Work, and how Gen Z describes what they do for a

---

1   Doing the same work for different employers is not a new concept, unlike holding the same job title across them.

living, will continue to specialise further as niche knowledge and skills become even more valuable to those who need them.

This is a double-edged sword for Gen Z. Those from older generations deep into their careers were able to identify both a specialism they could offer and unfulfilled demand. These people were in a strong position. They now have two to three decades of wider experience to draw upon. Gen Z does not have that level of experience and may be more restricted in what they can pursue.

If one specialism is all you need to get a business off the ground, that represents a lot less learning than an entire profession's worth. It also ensures there is time for the trends towards work-life balance and flexibility to grow further. As time goes on, and as new problems emerge that require solutions, Gen Z will have time to add strings to their bow.

Solopreneurialism will become ever more popular, whether as the sole form of work, or as additional elements of a work portfolio. The gig economy is not going away, but a sense of 'project economy' will emerge further, which offers a little more structure and stability. In short, 'gigs' will grow in size.

The ability for Gen Z to balance multiple part-time jobs or projects simultaneously will be particularly important[2], within a portfolio of hybrid or fully remote job arrangements.

The value of personal branding and online presence will only become more important, and reputation will remain significant. Having said that, there is only so much noise that anyone can tune into across

---

2   I might add this has some similarities with sixth formers balancing the demands of their teachers across a set of A level courses. This is an often-underrated aspect of studying at school.

social media, and the ability to form and maintain strong stakeholder relationships and build a client base from those you already know will remain important.

The key shift is that more Gen Z will have to engage in a portfolio career whether they wish to or not. This is for two reasons. One, the costs associated with addressing the climate crisis, whether through tax, inflation or insurance, will only increase and a single income will continue to be insufficient for too many in order to meet the cost of living. Two, as the value offered to organisations by the project economy grows, there will not be as much full-time work available. Similarly, the harder it is for organisations to find employees willing to work full-time and without flexibility, the less likely it is that they will offer full-time jobs as the default option.

If the worker they need is available right now, with a proven history of reliability and quality, with sufficient capacity to deliver what is required, why would companies go elsewhere? It may lead to an increase in labour costs, but a decrease in other costs associated with recruitment, retention, human resources and onboarding.

2. A lifelong education

As referenced earlier in the book, I used to deliver assemblies to secondary school students saying that the jobs they would do are yet to be invented. Years later, I found myself doing one of those jobs myself.

That has made me reflect on our education system and the principles upon which it is built. No school system can fully prepare its students for life given the accelerating speed at which life changes. Having said that, it can prepare students in dealing with the unpredictable and adapting to the paradigm shifts that will come their way. The system will need to become more effective in all aspects that are not represented in a set of qualifications. Schools will need to spend more time on them too.

I always used to work on the basis that you judge the effectiveness of a secondary school 10 years after its students have left. If anything, that is truer now than it was at the time. I am close to the 20th anniversary of when I started as a headteacher, and as I bump into former students, I have the opportunity to work out how well school prepared them for their thirties as well as their twenties.

Education will become ever more lifelong and less linear. Qualifications gained at school and university will still matter, but what happens next will matter at least as much. Job roles will require employees to engage in learning continuously, often on a just-in-time basis and frequently in small chunks.

The world ahead will require a greater level of agility and flexibility from both employees and employers. Individuals who can reinvent themselves on an ongoing basis to learn what is new will be highly prized.

The same applies to those who develop the programmes, courses and learning experiences for others. Schools, colleges and universities can expect individual institutions to rival them for offering qualifications and accreditations. This will also pose a challenge to the government if 'unofficial' qualifications prove to be more valuable than those on offer to school students.

3. Supply and demand for employees will shift

Given that birth rates rose for the second half of Gen Z, there will be a shift in supply and demand. Organisations will not find it quite so hard to recruit the young staff they need. Those young staff will not experience the buyers' market compared to those who came into the workplace in the late 2010s and early 2020s.

A couple of unfortunate trends may also persist, to the detriment of Gen Z. I say 'trends' at present because they feel like glimmers that have the potential to take hold.

The first of these is overstocking. This is when organisations appoint more young staff than they need in the expectation that some will not turn up, or prove to be unreliable when they do. I understand this to an extent, if a lack of supply means that an employee does not arrive for work on day one because they have had a better offer. However, I do not support it when done for reasons based on some of the myths addressed in this book. I envisage organisations engaging in this strategy will be found out very quickly. This is particularly the case if staff are given inappropriate or unethical reasons for failing probations.

The second related trend is when onboarding is effectively treated as the final part of selection. A group of employees are hired with the expectation, requirement even, that a number do not make it through their first six months. Anecdotally, I am starting to see a lack of patience amongst employers playing out in 'firings' for those deemed to be 'unprofessional' or 'entitled'.

I am not saying those employers must be wrong, or that none of their employees will fall into either of those categories. However, there is an ethical issue with treating onboarding as the final part of selection. Filtering out potential employees who do not have the attitudes you are looking for should happen before a job offer is made, rather than leaving a young professional with a stain on their CV that could have been avoided.

This shift in supply and demand may be to the benefit of those in public sector jobs where there is less scope to be flexible in terms of hours and location of work. Those roles may also become more popular among those who do not wish to contemplate the insecurity of the solopreneur life. Even with these jobs becoming more popular, Gen Z is still likely to continue to demand and expect suitable compensation for roles that lack flexibility of working hours and workplace.

4. Expect change as Gen Z become the politicians

The 2024 UK general election saw 10 Gen Z MPs returned to Parliament. One of them, Nadia Whittome, already had five years' experience having been elected in 2019. Maxwell Frost was elected to the US House of Representatives from Florida's 10th District in 2022.[3] Candidates must be over 25 to run for Congress, so the numbers are not as strong.

It will likely take at least couple of decades for Gen Z to become the most represented generation either side of the Atlantic. In advance of that, what can we expect they will champion?

a. Getting to grips with climate change

As the number of Gen Zers grows to the point that they can form a key voting bloc, their influence will increase. Given that Gen Z will live with the impact of climate change a lot longer than the previous generations who have amplified it, it is in their interests to see radical change on carbon emissions. The extent to which it will all be 'too little, too late' is another issue, not least because of the costs of ever more frequent extreme weather events.

---

3   No other Gen Z was elected to the US Congress in 2024. Madison Cawthorn was the next youngest at 29.

Expect government policy to increasingly encourage people to live in cities, where public transport and active travel can be the norm and green energy used more effectively. Urban farming and green spaces will be integrated more deeply into city planning.

b.   Serving Gen Z economic interests

The cost of living, and housing in particular, can only go so far, particularly as the population ages further. The cost of public services to meet this demand means they will become more expensive. Gen Z politicians will not expect the burden to rest with those in work. Expect a change in taxation systems towards capital as well as income, and a potential further rise in the pension age.

c.   Radical levels of transparency

The B-Corp revolution is just the start. B-Corps are expected to 'meet high standards of social and environmental performance, transparency and accountability'. Not every organisation will become a B-Corp. Apart from anything else, that would dilute the brand. Yet regulation will push businesses in this direction. Gen Z CEOs will prioritise social impact alongside profit as part of corporate social responsibility evolving into a core business strategy.

5. Mental health awareness and support will improve

The cost of poor mental health to the economy will have to be addressed in order to protect it. A country with a falling birth rate and ageing population cannot afford to have an ever-increasing proportion of adults who are not economically productive.
In time, therapy and mental health check-ups will be as routine for Gen Z as physical health check-ups were to older generations.

Workplace policies will need to express how they support mental health and work-life balance more explicitly, with examples to back that up. Employees will not expect organisations to wait for the right to disconnect to be enshrined in legislation before it becomes custom and practice. In 2025, 200 UK firms signed up for a four-day week[ii] with 'mental health and wellbeing' part of the rationale, along with increased productivity.

Expect mental health benefits and support systems to feature more strongly in employment packages and for burnout prevention to become a key management responsibility, as well as a core part of health and safety culture. Employees will not expect their employers to wait until the symptoms of burnout kick in before they act. Burnout, like retention, needs to be managed from the very beginning.

On a more structural level, the potential offered by artificial intelligence in enhancing health outcomes[4] will apply to mental health as much as physical. Healthcare will become more personalised and preventative as part of enabling issues to be resolved at the lowest possible level. This may, in theory, also lower costs. It may seem too fanciful to imagine that the UK's health can move to a more proactive and low-cost model. The reality of an ageing population, high rates of sickness absence[5], as well as the cost of chronic diseases like diabetes[6], mean that a new model will have to be found.

There is a further angle to this, which is the increased level of healthcare required to support a workforce with later retirement ages should they

---

4   I keep reading how significant this will be, but I am not yet sure of the outcomes. For one, it does not affect the extent to which individuals are inclined to look after their own health.

5   Up a third from 5.8 days to 7.8 days from 2019 to 2023 according to CIPD's report Health and Wellbeing at Work.

6   Currently 10% of the budget according to NHS England.

be able to retire at all. It seems inevitable that the move to qualifying for the state pension at 67 will only be a staging post over time for further gains to 70 and beyond. Government resources for healthcare will need to account for individuals deep into their seventies and older requiring a doctor's appointment to manage their return to work for issues that they may not have even visited for in the past.

6. The sharing economy will continue to grow

The main catalyst for the growth of the sharing economy, where people and groups share resources, goods, and services, was economic necessity. As tackling, and responding to, climate change becomes ever more expensive, sharing will expand to new areas of life, because it offers practical and efficient solutions.

Examples of this include:

a. Ownership of 'big ticket' items like property and vehicles.
b. Community-based care models for children and the elderly.
c. Living in flats and apartments to manage the cost of energy across residences.
d. Other shared living arrangements to manage the cost of rent.
e. Co-housing projects[7]
f. Popularity of public transport rather than private.
g. Subscription models expanding to cover more aspects of daily life, from clothing to appliances.

Although I am very sure there is good money to be made for some organisations in enabling all of this to happen, there is still scope for it to be more cost effective for those seeking respite from the cost of living.

---

7   This is not a Gen Z project but should form a template for all those which follow. I'm very proud to say that my mothers-in-law were part of the driving force for this amazing project. A model for all co-housing projects which follow. https://www.newgroundcohousing.uk/

The sharing economy also plays well to Gen Z's desire to reduce waste and provide spaces to connect with others.

Despite the 'triple lock'[8], the state pension falls well short of the average rent of a one bedroom flat without any of the associated costs.[9] For those who never bought or inherited property, the prospects of retiring are slim. The state pension may allow for someone to become part-time, or for responsibilities to be relinquished because they can afford to live on a lower salary.

As Gen Z gets older, their propensity to be resourceful will become even more important.

What's coming next for Gen Alpha?

It is early days for Generation Alpha. At the time of writing and by my earlier definition of a 15-year generation, a small proportion are in secondary school, half are in primary schools and the remainder are not yet born.

Given this, predicting the future for Gen Alpha is even more speculative. The oldest will get the attention first as they start to enter the workplace around the end of the 2020s. I will restrict predictions to the older half of the generation as they get to their late teens and early twenties and therefore eligible for work.

---

8   The 'triple lock' might be a phrase in common usage, but it is rarely explained. The triple lock is a policy that automatically increases the UK state pension each April based on the highest out of inflation, average wage growth and 2.5%. While it has been a policy that reflects the propensity 65+ to vote, it does not look so generous against the cost of living for those 65+ who cannot afford to retire.

9   In September 2024, it was £1,113 per month across the UK, and that does not even include London. The state pension, at the time of writing, is £959 per month.

1. They will be better prepared for the workplace

The current issues with recruitment and retention across workplaces, and particularly the historically low percentage of young adults who are economically active, will see a response in changes to the school curriculum. Work experience will become more popular again, perhaps aided by a new National Curriculum that will require at least one meaningful placement.

A broader post-16 curriculum will also focus on skills required for work in addition to academic qualifications. I would love to feel confident enough to say that, finally, our approach to academic, vocational and occupational qualifications will mature and find a better balance. There have been too many failed attempts to make it happen. Diplomas, T levels and apprenticeships have all come and gone to varying degrees. Resourceful members of Gen Z have often found their way despite rather than because of their education.

When I comment on the decline of apprenticeships, I often experience surprised looks, but the figures[iii] are dramatic. From 2015-16 to 2022-23, the number of 'total starts' for apprenticeships fell by approximately a third from half a million. Within that figure, the number of 'higher' (above A level standard) apprenticeships increased fourfold (27,000 to 112,000) and 'intermediate' (GCSE equivalent) fell by three-quarters (291,000 to 76,000). Now we have a 'national skill shortage'. Our nation's ability to sabotage its future economic prospects can be hard to watch.

Schools have a responsibility to prepare young people for the workplace. Government has a responsibility to ensure they can do so. Organisations also have a responsibility to engage in order to have a better chance of recruiting the workforce they need. I am not going to predict a golden future, but I do think there will be a positive shift in the relationship between all three of them. Schools badly need to be a beneficiary of such a relationship given the chronic recruitment and retention issues they have faced for some time.

2. The balance between demand and supply for employees will be in Gen Alpha's favour

There will be fewer Alphas than there are Zs. Obviously this is a complete cheat as it is already known.

The evidence to date is that birth rates have fallen consistently across the Gen Alpha years, albeit at different rates over time. The trend began with the tail end of Gen Z in 2008 – perhaps not so coincidentally, this was the year of the GFC. Other than 2015 and 2021, the birth rate has fallen in each year of Gen Alpha.

The implications for employers are significant. It will be harder to find the staff they need unless pay, and other terms and conditions, reflect the market conditions. Current issues around recruitment and retention may feel very small compared to what is coming down the line.

It is possible that developments in technology, and AI in particular, will mean that there will not be as many vacancies to be filled, but experience points the other way. New technology may have removed the need for many jobs of the past, but history shows that it also creates more roles than it eliminates.[10]

---

10   A small point for a very big topic. By 'history', I am referring to any point from the Industrial Revolution onwards. The new job may not be immediately available to replace the old one, of course, but as a general rule technology is a net creator of jobs.

3. Anticipate rebellion

Gen Alpha are principally the children of Millennials, the generation that bucked the trend by being better behaved than the one before. While I maintain that continued with Gen Z, it can only go on for so long. At some point a younger generation is going to want to push back and do what used to be described to me as 'natural'. Gen Z might be in for a shock.

This will coincide with their Millennial parents not wanting their children to be subject to the same pressures too many of them faced when they were young. As legislation finally starts to catch up with the bigger social media platforms, Gen Alpha has a better chance of experiencing a phone-free childhood[11], including a social-media-free adolescence and early adult life. If 'phone-free' is stretching it, then a less phone-based childhood is not.

This will create the opportunity to make mistakes, cut loose and enjoy a greater level of freedom. That includes from both their parents and grandparents, who will be much more tech-savvy than those who came before them.

There is also a less optimistic reason, and that is the aftermath of the pandemic. At the time of the first lockdown in 2020, fewer than half of the generation had been born. The other half was split relatively evenly between those already in school and those too young to attend.

After the lockdown periods eventually finished, the effects of the pandemic on early years and infant education became increasingly

---

11   Comparatively at least. I'm not suggesting it all goes in the bin, just that the young may be spared the worst effects as parenting kicks back on its domination.

clear. At that point, I still had a fair amount of ongoing education consultancy work. I have vivid memories of visiting primary schools and seeing more children arriving at school traumatised by their lockdown experiences. Education psychologists were run off their feet with early years cases dealing with children who were one or more of mute, not toilet-trained, unable to concentrate or could not form relationships with their peers.

Years later, issues relating to engagement in education continued to make the news. Attendance levels in schools were low and not budging, the numbers not on a school roll at all continue to rise and the systems to support children with special educational needs commonly described as collapsed or collapsing.[12] As Gen Alphas become teenagers and young adults, this is going to play out in how they spend their time, and what they do.

As has always been the case, the youngest generation in the workplace will be misunderstood, underrated and unfairly maligned by those who go before them. Despite all the Myths I have sought to address in this book, it is likely that Gen Z will demonstrate this too. The trend of those who are misunderstood going on to misunderstand will be with us for some time yet.

---

12 Frequently newspapers report that it is on the 'brink of collapse', whereas I refer to it in the past tense. I do not wish to diminish the heroic efforts of all involved, including schools and local authorities, but no one is coping with the demand or has the resources to do so. The fact that some are coming close to doing so is miraculous, and not an indication that the system or resources are in a good place.

Endnotes

i   Statista. (2024b, July 8). *Number of people using food banks in the UK 2008-2024.* https://www.statista.com/statistics/382695/uk-foodbank-users/

ii   Makortoff, K. (2025b, January 27). Two hundred UK companies sign up for permanent four-day working week. *The Guardian.* https://www.theguardian.com/money/2025/jan/27/two-hundred-uk-companies-sign-up-for-permanent-four-day-working-week

iii   House of Commons (2025, January) *Apprenticeship statistics for England* https://commonslibrary.parliament.uk/research-briefings/sn06113/

10

Leaving Your Legacy

Over the course of this book, I have said several times that Gen Z does not need Gen X, nor any other older generation, in order for their generation to survive and prosper. Despite that, we are in a position to support them to thrive.

Gen Z might be able to educate themselves, start a business, build an audience, a customer base and a portfolio career without depending upon older generations, but that does not mean all will do so, nor that they are all equally capable of making it happen. The model of learning at school, gaining a job from someone 20 years older than them, and staying in that line of work for life will not disappear completely. As I have said, the differences within any generation are far greater than those between them.

Despite their necessary self-sufficiency, you are still in a position to help. As the demographics kick in with more members of Gen Z in the younger half of the generation compared to the first, the supply and demand dynamics will change. It will be less of a buyers' market and organisations will be able to be more selective in who they employ.

If the older generations want health care, social care and pensions to be available for their autumn years, you need the younger generations to have more children and do it sooner. The birth rate will only increase if Gen Z can afford to have them. Facilitating that will require shifts in how the public finances are raised, and support from older generations for outcomes which will not immediately benefit them.

There is a tenuous argument that a lower birth rate will release the strain on public finances, as fewer need to be educated. Whatever public spending might be saved on educating fewer members of the nation's youth is greatly offset by the tax they will generate when they reach working age. You also need their offspring to become healthy, economically productive adults to maximise the return. And you need them to pursue employment in the public services that you will depend upon in time.

There is also more to the relationship between generations than matters relating to employment. This section will cover employment as well as families, and the roles of other adults whether parents, grandparents, aunts or uncles[1] from whichever generation they belong.

How best to leave your legacy?

1. Soft skills

Parents have a critical role to play in helping their children learn everything school does not teach them. 'As was ever thus' you might say, and I would agree. The triangular relationship between school, child and parents has always been of supreme importance across both the primary and secondary phases.

---

1   Apparently the collective term for aunts and uncles is 'avunculi'. You learn something new every day.

The difference in this day and age is that the internet, including social media channels, can and will fill much of this gap. This applies whether you wish it to be the case or not. There are three severe limits on the usefulness of this model.

The first is that some skills cannot be learned most effectively from some internet research or watching a collection of short videos. They might be helpful for broadening understanding, or as an initial introduction, but can also only go so far. They require guidance, practice and to be left alone to see if you can work out the next steps or not.

The second is that modern content can be extremely helpful in breaking down information and processes into a series of steps. The issue is what lies beyond those steps, including new and previously unencountered problems. Breaking down tasks and skills to multi-step processes is very helpful when appropriate, but life is not a walkthrough. I met someone after a talk who was really surprised that his daughter had used TikTok to work out how to cook rice, yet equally surprised that for the parts of the process not covered by the video, she was reluctant to work them out.[2]

Finally, the internet is also a source for deliberately misleading, inaccurate and vexatious content. The size of an audience for a video is a guide to popularity rather than quality. Gen Z, particularly at the younger end, does not have decades of experience in spotting the liars and fraudsters who used to market themselves using other methods and have now moved to social media.

Older generations had to figure out much more for themselves because the resources were not there. That does not mean that we were able to teach ourselves everything. In many cases we had

---

2   What else is there to work out about cooking rice? It turned out the unanswered questions included how much rice to use, whether to boil the water in a pan or a kettle, and how best to strain it.

access to books, newspapers and magazines that could provide similar information but in another format. As someone with very few practical or technical skills, I was always impressed with anyone who taught themselves to fix appliances, refurbish houses, had an innate sense of direction, or looked after gardens or woodland.[3] No book or video was going to help me make a start on very many tasks.

I find this kind of nostalgia is often exaggerated as it was often a parent, or other family member, who helped to get someone going with whatever it was. The young person had to take it from there. The point is that we did not expect to receive a complete picture, and would arrive at a point where we had to work it out for ourselves, rather than expect another video or 'PDF expert guide' to do the next bit for us.

Whether it is in terms of communication, teamwork, problem-solving, critical thinking, adaptability, time management or any other aspect of life, older adults have experiences to pass on and learning to share. This comes from the perspective of those who had, to some extent, worked it out themselves and accepted the risks of making mistakes along the way. The confidence that comes from correcting our own mistakes, and extricating ourselves from far worse, is not to be underestimated.

However you gained your life experience, it will be helpful. Supporting someone to generate some confidence that they can and will work it out for themselves is a great way to share it.

2. Supporting Gen Z to become parents

I am not a big fan of the comedian Jason Manford[4], but I did find

---

3   You might think this is a strange example, but I hear this a lot. Any wood keepers out there?

4   But then, who is? On the few occasions I visited the Buzz comedy club in Manchester when I lived in the area, I like to think he must have served me a few drinks at some point, since he worked behind the bar before he became one of the acts.

it amusing when he said that you get more instructions with an IKEA Billy bookcase than a baby. Even if the average age of becoming a parent continues to rise into the thirties, this does not mean that Gen Z will necessarily be any more prepared for parenthood.

As mentioned earlier, a lot of risk has been designed out of life compared to the experience of older generations. I suspect that this is part of the reason for the dropping birth rate, and the rise in the average age of the new parent. It is not all about the money or the state of the world, but also about financial constraints, fewer romantic relationships and a lower propensity to want to bring children into the world they experience.

The risks associated with having a young child, including the physical health of mother and child, and the various trials of infanthood, cannot be offset.

Gen Z's parents can provide the reassurance their sons and daughters need to start family planning and be present in the formative years of their child. To different extents, they can provide financial assistance along the way.

They can also support with the financial literacy to make it through the early years of parenthood, particularly when eye-watering sums of money disappear into childcare. Personal finance and budgeting are two topics that remain absent from the school education of far too many.

3. Scale up

As the figures from Companies House indicated in Chapter 4, the very significant rise in the formation of new companies has also been accompanied by a rise in dissolutions. The number of companies may continue to grow overall but, given that a proportion of these businesses are side hustles[5], there is likely to be a decent chunk of them that stay small or evaporate altogether when the intention was for them to grow.

In principle, any small business, whether a side hustle or not, has the potential to scale up into the main or only source of income. While the barriers to entry in starting a new business are very low, there is a big difference between getting going and scaling up.

While the processes involved in scaling up may be different for many businesses, particularly for those that are internet-based, the long hours, grit, resilience and energy remain the same. Not only can older generations relay their own experience, but those with the time can provide some of it too.

You can also help them to understand you and your peers as a market. Scaling up means broadening a customer base and selling more to them. Those with more spending power are the most valuable ones to reach.

The scaling-up process can involve some of the most difficult decisions or circumstances an organisation will ever make or face. They include the founder who is not cut out to be a CEO, the co-founder who does not wish to pursue the post-start-up journey, staying online or moving to bricks and mortar, seeking investment or taking on borrowing. They are not straightforward decisions, and have good arguments on both sides. Potential success, or failure, could be the consequence of going either way. Those from the older generations with the experiences of ups and downs have much to offer.

---

5   How many companies are side hustles, or just one amongst many
     in a portfolio? It is a good question and there is no easy way
     of knowing. I am working on the assumption that if a 'side hustle
     company' does not scale up, it is not a disaster if the main job
     remains in place.

4. Take climate change seriously

By this I mean that you show you are committed to limiting it in both your personal and professional lives. While it might be true that individual contributions can only be small, it is also the only (and therefore best) one you can make. Cut back on private transport, plastic and fossil fuels. Work out what a net-zero life would really look like to you and make it happen. Hold your peers to account to do the same.

Too few of my generation seem concerned about how we will be regarded as ancestors in the future. You can be an exception to the rule.

Your consumer choices can accelerate the transition to renewable energy sources or promote sustainable consumption and waste reduction practices. You can support stricter environmental regulations and policies, and get involved in local conservation efforts and biodiversity protection.

In short, you can be the member of the older generation who is seen as making a difference for the good of future generations.

5. Tackle inequality

As covered in Chapter 8, Gen Z is the most diverse generation so far. Alpha, Beta and so on are more than likely to continue that trend.

You can use your experience and expertise to dismantle the systemic discrimination, which exists in so many areas of society. I recognise there will be plenty who strongly disagree with that statement. This book is written by a middle-class, middle-aged, above-average-height, straight, non-disabled, neurotypical, privately educated white male. I have been on my own journey, and am still learning. The least you can do is to educate yourself more deeply with the arguments and evidence, and not settle for the polemic. You may yet become a champion for equity, diversity and inclusion in the workplace and across society.

At the very least, inform yourself. You may experience moments when you realise you need to unlearn some of the assumptions and biases that may have been with you for a very long time. The more you look, the more often that might happen.

Your support for policies that address wealth inequality and unethical global business practices can make a difference. You can also refer to the ample evidence that shows diversity is good for business.[i]

6. Mental health awareness and support

As a member of the older generation, you can do much to address the Snowflake Myth.

You can help to destigmatise conversations on the topic, and pull up those who seek to mock or ridicule. You can support improved access to mental health resources and treatment, not least because of the economic benefits to the nation of doing so. It is bad enough having a falling birth rate, but much more when the percentage of those who are not economically active continues to grow.

In your workplace, you can promote work-life balance and stress management techniques, and show that you value emotional intelligence.

You can also look after your own mental health, and model what it is to do so. Offering dialogue on your mental health can be empowering for others and open up a conversation that would otherwise have stayed shut. The same applies to being clear on what mental health means.

7. Volunteer

There are infinite possibilities when you decide to donate your time for free. You can revitalise a local community space, mentor a local business owner or bring your wisdom as a school governor. You could get engaged in politics as a councillor, or become a magistrate. These are all examples of where your informal and unpaid participation can have a significant positive impact on both individuals and the wider community.

As a mentor, you can work with those who represent the younger version of you, or support others whom life has not treated kindly.

The responsibilities of parenting, and grandparenting, can be considerable, but those who have retired can spread your influence so much wider. Remember that retirement may soon become a luxury rather than an entitlement. Your input might be fundamental to the success of others, and their life chances, not a mere added bonus.

8. Be their advocate

Older generations can use their networks, influence, voices and votes to support Gen Z's interests. You can put the priorities of the younger generation above your own, or support political solutions that do the same.

Out of a very long list of potential examples, you can support reforms for cheaper higher education, fair wages and worker protections, plus realistic criteria for 'affordable housing'. You can develop frameworks for responsible artificial intelligence and technology use. The latter includes online protections for young users of social media, and ensuring those platforms are held accountable for the content. You can protect them further by advocating for data privacy and digital rights.

I have had thousands of interactions over the course of writing this book and talking to audiences about Gen Z where I see people's eyes narrow that I might be on to something. You can help to spread this message. You really can make a difference in so many ways. Your actions can bring hope and positivity to others. You can improve your community and develop social cohesion.

Gen Z may not always know how you can help, or even that they need you at all. You can show them otherwise. We all have a responsibility to challenge the Snowflake Myth.

Endnotes

i   Dixon-Fyle, S., Hunt, D. V., Huber, C., Del Mar Martínez, M., Prince, S., & Thomas, A. (2023b, December 5). Diversity matters even more: The case for holistic impact. McKinsey & Company. https://www.mckinsey.com/featured-insights/diversity-and-inclusion/diversity-matters-even-more-the-case-for-holistic-impact

Acknowledgements

First and foremost, I want to thank my wife Sarah and daughter Lara who have tolerated me being shut away for many hours and days in the course of writing this book. Turning this from a hare-brained idea into reality has relied on their love and patience.

I also want to thank my mum and dad for all their support across my life, not least in recent years which have been an incredibly difficult time for the family. The book is dedicated to my sister Clare whom we lost in June 2024 after a long and stupendously brave battle with her health. My thoughts have been with her, my brother-in-law Mark and my nephews Finn and Innes throughout.

The process of writing a book has veered between feeling frivolous and vital during this period, and the support of family and friends has meant a lot.

I would like to thank my Virtual Assistant Shaheen Riaz who does all the important work in the background in order for me to concentrate on this.

A big thank you to Kris Emery. Without her editing services, this project would not have got off the ground, let alone to the point of publication. My learning curve has been steep and I am very grateful.

Thank you to everyone at Troubador Publishing for all their expertise and support in taking a Word document into its final formats.

Thank you to Shiggi Pakter from Audiofy for all support and endless patience with the audiobook. Thank you also to Sarah Short for pointing me towards Shiggi and all other connections and advice in recent years. Long live The Coaching Revolution!

I would like to thank leadership coach Sue Belton for her help in transitioning from behind the headteacher's desk to what I do today. Those first moves were so important.

A big thank you for everyone who has contributed in any other way. This includes all those who facilitated and participated in the focus groups, sent me links to articles, commented on my blogs, posts and videos on social media and every member of an audience who came to find me after my talk to tell me what resonated with them. I would also like to express gratitude for everyone who has booked me, and facilitated a booking, to speak.

There are many others who have supported me on my journey from secondary school headteacher to the freelance solopreneur I have become. I cannot name you all, but you know who you are, and thank you.

Finally, I would like to thank all the students who went through all the schools I worked in, from classroom teacher to headteacher. My determination for them to get a fair shake in life inspired me throughout my school career, and that will never diminish.

Further reading

I should emphasise that while I looked at hundreds of articles and blogs online, of which only a tiny fraction is represented here, I deliberately did not get into much of the existing literature. This was because I wanted to follow my nose and form my own conclusions, with my professional experience as a starting point.

These are books I have read either in the course of my research, or after I had drawn my conclusions. Deliberately, it is a small list and even within this there are some I paid more attention to than others. If you want one as a starting point, go to Jeanine Connor.

Jeanine Connor: *'You're not my f*cking mother' and other things Gen Z say in therapy*
Jason Dorsey and Denise Villa: *Zconomy*
Jonathan Haidt: *The Anxious Generation*
Corey Seemiller and Meghan Grace: *Generation Z, A Century in the Making*

Beyond that there is no shortage of articles and videos. Do what Gen Z would most likely do and search #GenZ on Tiktok.

Working with me

I offer a range of professional services. They include:

- Speaking at conferences and events. Topics include:
  - Recruiting and Retaining Gen Z.
  - Managing the Multi-Generation Workforce.
  - Understanding Gen Z.
  - See more at https://www.alexatherton.com/speaking.
- Staff training, including on the themes in this book.
- One-to-one leadership coaching – I specialise in working with senior leaders and CEOs in a range of industries. See more at https://www.alexatherton.com/coaching.
- Leadership team coaching – medium-to-long-term programmes to transform collective performance. See more at https://www.alexatherton.com/teams.
- Bespoke work and projects as requested.

Please reach out on LinkedIn, or email me directly at alex@alexatherton.com.